Educating the Urban Race

Educating the Urban Race

The Evolution of an American High School

Ericka J. Fisher

LEXINGTON BOOKS
Lanham • Boulder • New York • London

Published by Lexington Books
An imprint of The Rowman & Littlefield Publishing Group, Inc.
4501 Forbes Boulevard, Suite 200, Lanham, Maryland 20706
www.rowman.com

Unit A, Whitacre Mews, 26–34 Stannary Street, London SE11 4AB

British Library Cataloguing in Publication Information Available

Library of Congress Cataloging-in-Publication Data Available

ISBN 978-1-4985-0182-8 (cloth : alk. paper)

∞™ The paper used in this publication meets the minimum requirements of American National Standard for Information Sciences—Permanence of Paper for Printed Library Materials, ANSI/NISO Z39.48-1992.

Printed in the United States of America

For my family, particularly my parents Eliot and Joan, as well as my partner in crime and foe at times, my brother Jeffrey, for providing me with the care, unwavering support, structure, and discipline to persevere and develop resilience at a very young age. To my young family Brianna and Alexandra who beyond all else drive me to continue my social justice agenda. For the countless educators and mentors who have and continue to shape me in unquantifiable ways: Mark Hallihan, Patricia Rushton, Cynthia McMullen, Victoria Swigert, Ed Thompson, Robert Colbert, Meg Kursonis, Mark Freeman, Danuta Bukatko, and Helen Whall. You all have exemplified that care must come first, then, and only then, can knowledge be built.

Contents

Preface

"Can you please tell someone?"

These simple words scrawled onto the "additional comments" section of an anonymous bubble survey transformed the following study. My work began as an analysis of the programmatic changes implemented at one particular school. It became a mission to tell someone—to tell you—what I heard from urban adolescents who themselves speak for their public school peers across America.

My exploration of Burncoat Senior High School began, I suppose, as do many urban high school movies. A young, dynamic, dedicated, and charismatic principal sets out to implement changes that he hopes improve the dismal academic performance of his students. He begins with the ninth graders, placing them and groups of teachers in teams. His own training tells him that these "learning communities" should make a qualitative impact on student engagement and, by eleventh if not tenth grade, significantly improve achievement. My research focused on assessing the impact of this programmatic shift. I began with a simple, anonymous, pre and post survey of all ninth, tenth, and eleventh graders.

After the first year of implementation the results showed no significant shifts in student engagement. However, what the one hundred questions answered by hundreds of students did reveal was that something was happening at Burncoat Senior High. There were individual responses that spoke of amazing success; there were other responses that would leave any reader deeply troubled. While the statistical data could stand in isolation and cause those who read it to say "early days" and ask for patience, the statistical data would neither speak for these students nor do justice to Burncoat High. The statistics, moreover, might speak to my professional competence but they would not speak for me, for all that I witnessed while coolly assessing numbers.

My family is from Worcester, Massachusetts, the setting of this story. I am a product of its urban school system. I am a multiethnic woman who, having graduated from that public school system, furthered my education and now work as a tenured professor at a prestigious private college. My credentials are what won the trust of the officials who let me begin my study of Burncoat's attempts at reform. But when I spoke with students at Burncoat, they not so subtlety expressed shock at my story. How could I look like them or have grown up in their schools and be where I am today? Their shock made me wonder the same thing. What had made the difference?

My memories of my own educational experiences begin in daycare. I liked daycare. I thrived on the attention, on the activities. By the end of second grade I was fighting to survive in an urban, crowded, complex school. I vividly recall being bullied and fighting back. My defenses heightened, I arrived at school every day ready for battle but intellectually disengaged. At the end of my second grade year, my parents enrolled both my brother and myself in parochial school. Within three months I was transformed. The truth is, I was safe. I had structure. I was free to focus on learning. I was back in the kind of "day care" that makes students love rather than dread or merely endure school.

My parents, however, remained strong advocates of public education, firm believers that we should find there the care we needed in order to learn. I returned to public school in seventh grade strong, resilient, and ready to take on the challenge. Of course, I also knew that my grandmother worked in the main office. Nobody was going to risk getting my grandmother on their backs. My family was vitally engaged in my education throughout the tumultuous adolescent years. My father routinely lectured my brother and me with the words, "This family comes first, your education is second, and right now nothing else matters." His words have become my mantra as a parent.

When my older brother started his junior year of high school, my dad brought home a filing cabinet. He labeled the draws for my brother and myself and then filled them with college applications. When the time came, my parents took my brother up and down the East Coast looking at colleges; when it was my turn, I sat in the backseat rolling my eyes all the way to my prospective institutions of higher learning. Not many of my school friends had to go through this rite of passage so I figured I might not fit in at college. My parents were not taking that as an excuse. I decided I would try it for a semester. Within two weeks, I was so in love with the classroom that I knew I would never stop learning. Never in a million years did I think I would become a teacher, though. You see, there was this small matter of justice.

Given what I had seen during my first eighteen years of life, I assumed that if I wanted justice, if I wanted to make change in the world, I would literally need to work within the justice system.

During my senior year of college, I interned for a battered women's organization, helping women navigate the court system. Upon graduation, I entered a PhD program in order to study criminology. When the program seemed to be more about justice in theory than about achieving justice, I dropped out and took the police exam. I was recruited by several departments. Then, and they now know of my gratitude, a few wise counselors asked me to take time before making another decision I might undecide.

Much to my parents' dismay, I became a receptionist at the University of Massachusetts. On my lunch breaks, I would go door to door in various departments speaking with professors. One day, I stumbled into Professor Robert Colbert's office and I told him my story. I told him I wanted to help make children's lives better and that I wanted justice. That afternoon, we spoke of how punishment appropriate to a crime is often meted out by the criminal justice system and that such action does achieve a kind of justice while making communities safer. But quietly, patiently, Professor Colbert made me think about what could possibly bring justice to children? I remember him smiling as it dawned on me that the cliché earned its way to being a cliché by being true: education can be the great equalizer. I had found my vocation. I enrolled in the University's School of Education and never again felt I had veered from the path of justice. I did, however, learn that education becomes the great equalizer only if provided to all children carefully and equitably.

Good. I had a justice agenda. Improve the American public school system. But that still didn't explain why I had become who and what I was. I began, for reasons then not clear to me, to focus on the impact of trauma on childhood learning. During my graduate training, I also learned that even good, equitable education can become inaccessible to traumatized children. We see children as "resilient." We become hardened to the routine cruelties children inflict on other children. We, the adults, shake our fingers at parents who may neglect their children's homework but ignore the traumas those children endure that may well make it impossible for them to engage with schoolwork at home or in class. And that was the key. It wasn't just that my parents took an active interest in my education that mattered. It was their insistence on my safety. It was their day in, day out demonstration of care, of vigilance, that made me feel safe enough to fall in love—as children at play so often will—with learning. My work now focuses on the psychological and socio-emotional needs of students if they are to learn. Which brought me to a very different understanding of what I was reading in those comment sections on those Burncoat assessment sheets.

The stories of the urban high school known as Burncoat, of the students who sometimes prosper and often fail there, and of the community that houses them all are much more complex than statistics can ever reveal. Those stories needed to be told in context and in relation to each other. Then the statistics would also matter. I sat down to write my book.

Writing this book with an eye toward doing justice for the children has been my greatest challenge for I eventually realized that I might not seem to be doing justice to the many teachers and administrators who had given me access to their school and their work for eight long years. I also knew I owed much to the Burncoat neighbors and parents who spoke with me freely. But truth is the prerequisite for justice and I have striven here to preserve factual truth in all areas other than the naming of children. The name of the city and its schools are not altered in any way. Names of public officials and matters of public record are written as such. However, names and identifying features of students have been altered in order to protect the privacy and confidentiality of minors. In order, and I do not say this lightly, to spare them trauma.

Introduction

"urbs urbis"

When asked what image springs to life when the word urban is mentioned words such as "crowded," "street corners," and "poverty" are often offered by my undergraduate students. What image do you mentally concoct when you hear the word "urban"? Is it a romanticized image of museums, restaurants, and all the accoutrements that come with being an urbanite? Or rather is it an image of despair and desolation, one of poverty and crime? Read the following sentence and close your eyes for a moment. What image springs to life when you see the words "urban student"? Do you see urban students as those that live in urban areas and populate the elite private schools, picked up and quickly whisked away by caregivers at the end of the day for various lessons and social events? Or is your impression one of students attending failing schools? What languages do the students you imagine speak? What are their ethnic backgrounds? Or is it as simple as Weeks points out "We all know an urban place when we see it" (Weeks 2010, 33). Why is it that when a college aged student or twenty-something suggests they want to go to university in the city or spend a few years after graduation in the city before having a family it is seen as an adventure or something expected for this demographic? However, to raise a family in the city, to have children who attend the public schools, is often seen as questionable or at worse, neglectful in some way.

For America's children, for students, growing up urban has become a tainted label. This label weighs them down as surely as an anchor tethers a ship to the ocean floor. Imagine that ship anchored to the ocean floor in a storm, unable to sail out of the chaos—the ship is unforgivingly battered and abused. When the storm passes the ship has sunk to the ocean bottom alongside its anchor. America's urban student, much like that ship, is tethered to "urban education" or the "urban school system." This system, its teachers, funding, and reputation are being battered by a storm. The anchor, the school system, is sinking to the bottom; the child, the student with so much promise and potential, is now being dragged to the bottom alongside the mechanism that was intended to anchor them. The educational system that was intended to provide stability as they grew into productive citizens now has betrayed America's children simply by association. By acquiring one simple label "urban" the urban student has become the other, illegitimate, different from the norm. The urban student has indeed been bastardized in America.

How did the term urban become such a powerful weapon and tool used to oppress those who acquire the label? Utilizing intersectionality theory I will argue "Urban" came to be the weapon of choice due to the intersection of three very powerful variables: ethnicity, socioeconomic status, and social capital. When these three variables, and weapons of oppression in isolation, come together in a particular pattern the individual, or for the purposes of this text, the student can now be identified as belonging to the Urban race. Thus, low socioeconomic status, limited social capital, and particular ethnic identifiers together culminate in the Urban label.

The theoretical framework of intersectionality arose from feminist scholarship. While that point is generally agreed to by researchers there is some concern as to how this framework is being applied in sociological research. It is a framework traditionally utilized in the study of gender, specifically as a methodological approach applied to the study of inequality. Choo and Ferree (2010) argue that intersectionality is not just "crossing paths" rather it is dynamic and as such is transformative, thus a powerful tool for researchers. Through their analysis of intersectionality Grant and Zweir offer that "reading of the literature suggests that identity axes interact to produce oppression and privilege in schools, so intersectionality analyses and practices should be part of our toolbox for increasing student achievement" (Grant and Zweir 2011, 182). Intersectionality is important because it focused "attention on the vexed dynamics of difference and the solidarities of sameness in the context of antidiscrimination and social movement politics. It exposed how single-axis thinking undermines legal thinking, disciplinary knowledge production, and struggles for social justice" (Cho, Crenshaw, and McCall 2013, 787). In the context of contemporary schooling intersectionality is powerful as it is a methodological tool which can be utilized to give voice to the oppressed, examine the intersections of multiple identities, as well as examine both sameness and difference amongst populations.

It is indeed the intersection of three constructs: race/ethnicity, socioeconomic status, and social capital that combine to oppress the Urban student. Morning categorizes racial conceptualization as a "cultural grouping, biological entity or social construct" (Morning 2009, 1184). The concept of race is one which varies individual to individual and is often fluid. Indeed, one's concept of race may rest in any of the three categories mentioned above or as a combination at any time. Walsemann, Bell, and Maitra (2011) posit ". . . schools play a complex role in the social and cultural reproduction of social inequalities. They can also act as racializing agents, shaping the worldview of their students." Furthermore, "such information is conveyed through the power structure within the schools, the use of racial code words by school personnel and parents (e.g., 'urban,' 'dangerous')" (Walsemann, Bell, and Maitra 2011, 1873). Socioeconomic status (SES) is a widely used variable in the social sciences and includes three components: family income, parental education, and occupational status/prestige. SES is seen to have an impact on child outcomes in multiple domains including the educational setting (Bradley and Corwyn 2002). The final construct, social capital, can be defined as "the sum of the resources, actual or virtual, that accrue to an individual or a group by virtue of possessing a durable network of more or less institutionalized relationships of mutual acquaintance and recognition" (Bourdieu and Wacquant 1992, 119). Social capital can be simply viewed as the benefits associated with an individual's membership in a particular network. All three of these constructs will be discussed at length in future chapters.

The term urban is bandied about with very little agreement on definition. The term "urban" should not provoke anxiety and fear. "Urban" is derived from the Latin "rubs urbis," the word for "city." John Weeks writes of urban areas as "being a characteristic of place rather than of people" (Weeks 2010, 33). Authors Rury and Hill point out that by 1961 the term urban was already linked to race as White flight to suburbs increased and metropolitan schools became increasingly "Black" (Rury and Hill 2012). Dyan Watson suggests that both the terms urban and suburban, specifically as they relate to education, are loaded with values, beliefs, and stereotypes. In Watson's examination of novice teachers there was a clear majority that wanted to teach in urban schools but did not want to teach Urban students. Using the terms "urban, but not *too* urban" or "urbanesque" to define their ideal setting. The conclusion drawn was that these novice teachers wanted to work with students of color, but those who resembled their image of suburban students with suburban resources (Watson 2011). Ultimately, many wish to teach the Obama "type" minority, not the others.

I would take the suggestion that urban has become inextricably linked to race one step further and propose that it has become a socially constructed category in its own right that serves to disempower all those who self-identify or are labeled as such. Just as racial and ethnic qualifiers have historically served to segregate, oppress, and justify inequality so too does the label of urban, particularly as it is applied to vulnerable populations such as children. The Urban (capital U) student is now seen as different from the norm and that norm is suburban. The Urban student is seen as one who attends failing schools, with bad teachers, uninvolved parents, and violent peers. Labeling students as Urban affords society the ability to justify the hierarchal nature of public schooling, wherein suburban reigns supreme and Urban is destined to failure. It affords society, liberals, neoliberals, and conservatives, the ability to have little empathy when "those" Urban schools produce millions of children every year who do not reach their fullest potential; as Urban student failure is seen as predestined and a fait accompli. The classification of Urban allows society to give up on these children whereas if many of the injustices experienced by the Urban student were to be experienced in suburbia a true social movement would ignite and be difficult to extinguish until all children (in suburbia) received the education deemed fit for suburban students. Indeed, American society has created a new minority group. Unfortunately for America this minority group will be a majority minority group and as this group continues to fail the implications for American society are dire.

The structure of this book seeks to give the reader a series of rich contexts in which to understand how the American Urban student and Urban school came to fruition. Through the use of data and various frameworks the reader will get a comprehensive understanding of the many factors at play. The first framework is historical. Chapter 1, entitled "The Foundations of a School System," brings the reader back to the 1600s and the Colonial roots of the Worcester Public School system, indeed one might argue the roots of American education. Schools have histories and these histories predate the physical structure of the school building. By examining the foundations, both philosophical and structural, of the Worcester Public School system, the reader can gain a general understanding of what the community of Worcester hoped for from their school system. We also begin to see how some issues continue to be pervasive and contentious hundreds of years later.

Chapter 2, entitled "Neighborhood Matters," explores the community in which the high school at the center of this book is housed. A neighborhood has the potential to build and support its school or the neighborhood can negatively impact the functioning of the school. The corollary is also true: a school can have a tremendous impact on the neighborhood by serving as the mechanism that solidifies or fractures a community. Chapter 2 exemplifies these points in relation to Burncoat Senior High and the surrounding community. Again, here I engage with specifics but the underlying lesson of how and why a neighborhood matters everywhere is exemplified by Worcester.

Chapter 3 brings the reader into Burncoat, the only possible title for this section of the book. This portrait of an urban high school comes from a very specific yearbook: 2010–2011. The chapter examines the specific city, state, and national educational policies as well as the demographics and temporal events that could be documented that year. The picture is one of a very particular school in a very particular time. However, just as the portraits of graduating seniors take on remarkable similarity as photographic layouts trend across the country, so too is my depiction of a case study of American urban education. If we were to remove the name of the school, the data reflects much of what we are seeing in postindustrial, urban centers around the nation. History tells us, moreover, that in all due time what we see in urban centers will transcend boundaries and become matters of importance to suburbia as well. Therefore, to look at Burncoat through the lens of social theory is to bear witness to the challenges facing American public education itself.

In succeeding chapters entitled "The Complexity of Race and Socioeconomic Status" and "The Importance of Relationships," I unpack the data and bring in the voices of the students at Burncoat. As adults, we accept on a cognitive level that the constructs of race, socioeconomic status, and relationships are complex and convoluted. Nevertheless, educational professionals such as teachers and administrators within a school are expected to balance these complex constructs effortlessly while educating the masses. Better yet, they are expected to do what our society as a whole has failed to accomplish: process, then transcend these factors so that all students become citizens of a truly post-racial institution. In this fabricated utopian post-racial system our educational professionals are expected to get to a state where neither race, socioeconomic status, or interpersonal relationships matter.

Why? Quite simply, because teachers are hired to educate, to transmit knowledge. Those other factors simply should not matter; therefore they do not matter. Except when they do, which is when the educator is blamed for failure to educate and transmit knowledge. Because race, socioeconomic status and interpersonal relationships all walk right in with the students who bare their weight. We see, as later chapters will argue, utopian assumptions at play in educational policy; all schools must meet the same standards, no excuses. No excuses for age, either. What is challenging for adults must also be processed constructively by the students within the school. Children, and sixteen-year-olds are children, must process and then often attempt to mitigate the losses or capitalize on the benefits associated with their race, socioeconomic status, and relationships without acknowledging that these factors matter. This is the plight of those who try to navigate the turbulent waters of our urban public schools and this is the plight of the children for whom the adults so valiantly attempt to aide in their navigation.

The story of urban education has been told in many ways. Dedicated and passionate authors and educators such as Kozol, Noguera, Ayers, and Delpit have put the spotlight on the conditions in which our society's underserved populations are being educated, while Meier and DelPrete speak of great successes achieved with school reform. More recently Diane Ravitch has put forward a history of reform efforts, documenting the successes and failures.

I have attempted to bring the observations of these scholars to the uniquely paradigmatic case of Worcester and of Burncoat. I anticipate that the educational professionals and future educational professionals who read this book will recognize in it not only the challenges but also the great potential and joys brought by working in urban schools with urban students and partners. Cities, this book hopes to remind its readers, were built not just to house labor but to render accessible museums and theaters and parks; to make accessible seats of government and medical centers; to celebrate institutions of "higher" learning. Urban public schools, like their students, are resilient. However, we must begin the process of reclaiming our schools and caring for our children. If we recognize their trauma, if we intervene and make America's schools once again a safe place to be young, we will have gone further than any industrial giant to revitalize our cities. But the work will take many hands and true collaboration.

President Obama utilized his 2013 inaugural address to specify the need for Americans to come "Together we resolve that a great nation must care for the vulnerable and protect its people from life's worst hazards and misfortune." There are numerous stakeholders in public education. There are students, families, community members, administrators, and school staff. There are entire school committees and much abused teacher unions. The number and diversity of the stakeholders might make coming together appear to be an insurmountable goal. But the story of Burncoat is, finally, a cautionary tale. We must unite. Can we? My final chapter is called "The Fight for Survival." It considers the very important roles each stakeholder must play while also suggesting the personal agendas that will need to be sacrificed. It begins with acknowledging the bastardization of the Urban school. Without this we will surely continue our Urban race to the bottom.

Chapter 1

The Foundations of an American Urban School District

The roots of education are bitter, but the fruit is sweet.

—Aristotle, translated by C. D. Yonge, 1853

In 2012, Worcester, Massachusetts, a metropolitan city, had a little over 180,000 residents. The center-state city whose slogan is "The heart of Massachusetts" won the All-American City award on five separate occasions. Home to ten colleges and universities, nearly 40 percent of all jobs in the city are in the education and medical fields (City of Worcester 2012). In 2012, Worcester was also named the second happiest place to work in the country by a study commissioned by *Forbes Magazine* (Smith 2012). In addition, Worcester was named one of the top five housing markets in the country for 2012 (Worcester Regional Chamber of Commerce 2012). Historically, Worcester's commitment to education and growth has not been quite so robust—indeed the origins of Worcester's educational system, like the origins of Worcester's economic system were tumultuous at best.

In keeping with its utility as an American paradigm, Worcester was originally an agricultural center. As the original colonies emerged as states, Worcester became a mill and factory town though its expertise was in the "light industry" of making household abrasives, then tool and die manufacturing, followed by the manufacture of pharmaceuticals. Worcester's evolution as a metropolis thus provides an intriguing case study of the evolution of an urban school system from the onset of the American nation. This chapter will chart the Worcester Public School District's early development.

Although it is difficult to imagine anything seemingly less urban than the pilgrims, the story of urban education in the United States begins with the 1620 settlement of Plymouth, Massachusetts, by the first pilgrims followed

1

by the arrival of Puritan settlers in 1630. Over the next twenty years, there was great population growth that spread from the shorelines of Massachusetts into the interior of the state. The early Puritan settlers were predominantly dutiful farmers who relied heavily on agricultural production for sustenance and survival. However, as more settlers arrived and opportunities for economic growth were established, it did not take long for a class split to develop in the new land. This came in the form of the rising merchant class differentiating itself from the farmers within Puritan communities.

In Massachusetts, Puritan villages typically consisted of privately owned homes and farms surrounding the public common that held the central meetinghouse. Indeed, the meetinghouse and the pastor were the nucleus of the Puritan village. With no pervasive government at this time, the meetinghouse served as the location for the townspeople to congregate, hold town meetings, and make communal decisions. These town meetings are largely viewed as the foundation of American democracy. However, history also notes that town meetings were more productive in terms of maintaining conformity amongst the population rather than giving voice to the masses. For example, Puritan exclusionary practices assured that only men—and men who were property holders—were able to participate in said meetings. England, of course, had made the preeminence of male property holders a standard practice during the time period. But formalizing this mandate in a new land that had been sought for reasons of religious freedom afforded wealthy property owners even more power over a colonial village population. Now distant from any court or parliamentary control, the property owners' voices dictated the norms of the village, including decisions regarding education (Simmons 1968).

THE DEVIL MADE ME DO IT

Fortunately for the development of American society, even wealthy members of the early Puritan society viewed the development of schools as a pivotal step in building and maintaining strong community. Schools and educational facilities were seen as a fundamental community resource that would afford individuals an opportunity to study religion and the scriptures, habits that would in turn preserve and transmit the culture and expected norms of Puritan society. For precisely these reasons, "The Commonwealth of Massachusetts" established the Boston Latin School in 1635; one year later Harvard was established (Watras 2008). In alignment with Puritan beliefs, in 1642 a law was enacted that required parents to make certain their children knew both religious principles and the laws of the Commonwealth. Despite the emergence of the Latin School and Harvard College the law did not stress the role of formal education. The general belief was that transmission of cultural and religious mores could be fostered within the home. That being said, over the next five years, tensions in the Commonwealth rose as the Puritans became increasingly concerned that transmission of these norms and values were not passed on within all homes. A widespread fear that a whole generation of scripturally illiterate men was emerging engendered concerns over the society's ability to survive. Thus, in 1647, the General Court of Massachusetts introduced the Old Deluder Satan Act. The act's dubious name reflects its creators' core belief that by not educating man or making him literate, the old deluder Satan could thereby lead man astray. The 1647 act was a direct result of what many viewed as a distancing of settlers from core religious beliefs and more specifically parental negligence of the requirements outlined by the 1642 law (Eberling 1999).

The Old Deluder Satan Act required every town with a population of more than fifty families to provide a common school that provided instruction in reading and in Bible studies. During the Colonial era, a common school was by and large a classroom in a home that educated a number of children in heterogeneous groupings. The students were typically between the ages of five and fourteen. If the town had more than one hundred families, the town was also legally compelled to move beyond the common school and provide an additional school that would, as did the Latin School, prepare students for Harvard. This foundational education was not free. Parents or masters of children were responsible to pay for this education although there is some language in the act that suggests the town as a whole could pay for schooling (a precursor to local taxes being used to fund public education).

Thus, the Old Deluder Satan Act marks the first step toward compulsory education in the United States. The various towns throughout Massachusetts responded in a myriad of ways to this educational mandate, though each response was largely predicated on the prior education of the settlers and the agricultural demands of the land. In this regard, the British settlement of Worcester, originally called "Quinsigamond," takes on added dimensions of American heritage. The relevant land was originally occupied by members of the Nipmuc nation. In 1673, English settlers arrived and named the settlement "Quinsigamond" Two years later, when King Philip's War began between Native Americans and the English colonists, the settlement (then consisting of fewer than ten houses) was abandoned. In 1713 what was once Quinsigamond became the settlement of Worcester (Lincoln 1862). In 1722, seventy-five years after the 1647 law and nine years after the official settlement of Quinsigamond, Worcester, Massachusetts, was incorporated as a town.

The first evidence of the establishment of formal education in Worcester came three years after the incorporation during a December, 1725 town meeting. Reports from that assembly record the question of formal education

being raised "to See if ye Town will take Efectual Care & provide a writ-
ting School to Instruct ye Youth in Sd Town" (Worcester Historical Society
1722–1739).

DEFIANCE

A proposal to provide writing instruction for the youth of Worcester was put
forward and, in 1726, a proclamation was made by the townspeople: "We
y e Subscribers Doe hearby Covenant & agree with mr. Jonas Rice to be y
e Schoole master for S d Town of Worcester and to teach puch Children &
Youth as any of y e Inhabitents Shall Send to him : :o read & to write as y
e Law Directs, &c : And to keep Such Schoole untill y e fifteenth Day of
December next Ensuing y e Date tiearof : S d Schoole to [be] Suported at
the Towns Charge" (Worcester Historical Society 1722–1739). In order to
comply with this proclamation, the first permanent settler of Worcester, Jonas
Rice, became the initial schoolmaster of the first schoolhouse at the town's
expense. This rudimentary form of public education consisted of children
attending school in his home for reading and writing instruction from April
1726 to December 15, 1726.

On December 19, 1726, only four days after the completion of their initial
foray into formal education, the settlers of Worcester voted to discontinue
this instruction. The reasoning of the settlers although shortsighted was quite
practical in nature. The geographical location of Worcester made farming
particularly difficult. Worcester's high altitude and hilly terrain made winters especially brutal; snow often began in early fall and extended well into
spring. The townspeople recognized that the town and its residents were
better served if children assisted with the demanding agricultural work that
sustained the town rather than sit in a classroom. The governing authorities
of the Commonwealth did not agree with Worcester's assessment, and the
following year a fine was meted out to the town of Worcester by the colonial
government for failing to comply with educational law. The townspeople
responded to this action by voting and allocating town money to pay the fine
rather than utilize funds to comply with the law. And yet, though paying
the fine afforded a short term solution, the fine also spurred more discussion within the town meetings regarding education in the town of Worcester
(Daughters of the American Revolution 1903).

Recognizing the inability to subvert Commonwealth law, in 1727, monies
were appropriated by the townspeople of Worcester for a schoolmaster to
rotate between small home schools located in the various quadrants of town.
Two years later, in 1729, some townspeople expressed an increased desire to
build a school; however, during a town meeting, the majority of those who

held power—that is, the majority of male property owners—voted not to build. As of 1731, the town now had over one hundred families and as such encountered another regulation regarding formal education. In principle, the town was required by the Commonwealth and the Old Deluder Satan Act to move beyond the small home schools and provide grammar schools. In an attempt either to meet or subvert the legal requirements and avoid another fine, in 1731, the townspeople of Worcester voted to hire five additional schoolteachers. This vote and subsequent actions neither advanced the town beyond the small home schools nor distracted the Commonwealth. Since Worcester did not meet the requirements under the General Court of the Commonwealth, the town was again fined. In 1733, the townspeople—or more rightly, the town's wealthiest men—grudgingly relented and voted to build the first common schoolhouse in order to comply with Commonwealth law and avoid additional monetary penalties (Nutt 1919).

THE FIRST COMMON SCHOOL

Funded largely by donations, Worcester's first common schoolhouse was completed in 1738. The building, twenty-four feet by sixteen feet, was located in the middle of present day Lincoln Square. The citizens of Worcester hoped this schoolhouse would alleviate the educational scrutiny they had faced for years from the Commonwealth. Much to their chagrin, once again in 1745 Worcester and its people were criticized by the Commonwealth for not having a grammar school. (During this historical period the term "grammar school" referred to a school that prepared students for college and university, much like present day secondary schools.) Worcester's growing population and steadfast decision not to build a grammar school was regarded as shortsighted and a danger to the healthy development and economic competitiveness of the Commonwealth. Therefore, the Commonwealth continued to pressure the town.

Seven years later, Worcester again relented. Worcester's first Latin Grammar School, located near Main and Mechanic Streets, came to fruition in 1752, fourteen years after the legal requirement. The future second president of the United States, Harvard graduate John Adams, was scouted by Worcester town leaders at his Harvard commencement and came to Worcester in 1755 to become the first recorded head of the Worcester Latin Grammar School, which in 1845 will become Classical and English High School, located in the Lincoln Square building (Nutt 1919). Various documents suggest that John Adams struggled as a teacher. He had great difficulty with maintaining authority and control in the classroom. Not much older than many of his students, he was challenged at every turn. As noted earlier, Worcester experienced harsh winters with several feet of snow falling in multiple winter storms. The older male students used this act of nature to their advantage by attempting to throw future President Adams into the massive snow banks on several occasions (Daughters of the American Revolution 1903). It is clear that future President Adams experienced frustrations regarding classroom management to which many of our present day novice teachers could easily relate, and which reflect as well then as they do now, differing attitudes toward education fostered by the distinctions of locale. Worcester was becoming a city but one that functioned according to its own economic priorities. John Adams only stayed for three years teaching at the Latin Grammar School. Shortly after his departure, in clear defiance of the Commonwealth, the town deemed the school unsuccessful and subsequently voted to return to the moving home schools model created before the permanent grammar school was built.

Worcester's educational problems persisted into the post-Colonial era. In 1785, a grand jury noted that the town was seriously neglecting school affairs. At this time, a group of concerned citizens reorganized the school district (Daughters of the American Revolution 1903). Also, in the broader educational context during these years, Thomas Jefferson was urging schools to avoid the fanaticism of religion; this would have a lasting impact on American education. Jefferson felt this fanaticism was dangerous to the nation. He vehemently held the belief of religious and educational freedom and that taxes should not be used to support the teachings of mandated religion. His words began to permeate the nation and as such began to change what was once the primary purpose of schools in America (Peterson 1984). It is also important to note that the United States Constitution in 1776 and the various amendments that followed drastically limited schools' role in socializing children in the ways prescribed and outlined during the foundational years of American public schooling. The controversy surrounding the socializing purpose of schooling made notable by Jefferson in the 1700s can still be seen in current court actions against school districts, for example, *Smith v. Board of School Commissioners*, 1987; *Mozert v. Hawkins County Board of Education*, 1987; *Elk Grove Unified School District et al. v. Newdow et al.*, 2004. Although the blatant transmission of religious morality waned over the past two hundred years, remnants of early American education remain in the hidden curriculum of our present day schools; this sometimes not so hidden curriculum in schools pose philosophical divides amongst educational stakeholders.

NEW LAWS SAME PROBLEMS

In 1789 Massachusetts passed a law that followed up on the Old Deluder Satan Act and required free schooling and established school districts.

By 1800 there were ten schoolhouses in the town of Worcester. Nevertheless, in 1823, ninety-seven years after the district's first admonitions by the Commonwealth, the district's schools still remained well below general Commonwealth standards. In an effort to advance the school district and have a controlling body, this same year the Worcester School Committee was formed, the first such committee in the United States. Within a year of the Committee's formation, in 1824, Worcester voted to have schooling funded by local taxes rather than voluntary contributions. The powerful combination of the creation of a formal school committee and local taxation for education brought in a new era of educational development in Worcester (League of Women Voters 1964).

In Massachusetts, two other noteworthy educational developments transpired in the 1830s. First, the Board of Education was developed and Horace Mann became the first secretary of the State Board of Education in 1837. Horace Mann was a lawyer by training and also served in the Massachusetts state legislature before being nominated to become the secretary of the Board of Education. Mann was not a politician and therefore, he had very limited political power. However, he was diligent in his educational research and made his reports and findings available for public consumption. These reports were considered extremely valuable and were used by districts and schools in an attempt to improve education for students. Mann viewed education as imperative for the economic growth of the nation, and he worked tirelessly to acquire funds and resources to support public education. During his tenure Mann visited many schools and was struck by the inequity in educational resources afforded to children based on socioeconomic status. He noted the inadequate and sometimes dangerous facilities as well as the outdated educational materials imposed upon students and he sought a leveled approach to education (Cremin 1957).

Mann pushed for the common school. The common school would provide a uniform education that would be free to all children of the state of Massachusetts. Mann viewed education as ". . . the equalizer of the conditions of men, the great balance wheel of the social machinery" (Mann 2010). These common schools would be funded by taxes, this fundamental financial clause drew great opposition from many as it was seen as problematic to make citizens pay for all children to be educated even if they were not one's own children.

Mann held steadfast to his beliefs. He had become greatly disillusioned during his law practice and argued that it would be the school and education that would rid society of evil and crime, not lawyers. Indeed, the school-teacher would be a more powerful force against societal deviance than any police regime. In order for the education system to benefit all of society Mann argued for equitable education for all. However, all did not truly mean all children. Mann did not see a problem with the fact that the common schools he was promoting were largely Protestant based and therefore seemingly biased against the large number of Irish Catholic immigrants. In addition, African American children were also still educated in segregated schools, if educated at all (Mondale and Patton 2001).

SEGREGATION

Educational segregation was and continues to be a divisive subject in the United States. Who should be taught, where and how they should be taught, was also a topic of great debate during the early formation of public schooling. During this historic time African Americans were thought by many to have different innate intellectual and cultural needs thus requiring a different education. African American families often did not send their children to these early free schools fearing ill treatment by teachers and white students. Although seemingly contradictory to what is seen as a general opposition to segregation by African Americans, as early as 1798 African American families petitioned the Boston School Committee for a segregated school, and it was the committee that initially refused. However, in 1806 the school committee relented and established a separate school for African American children. In less than fifteen years' time it became clear that the black schools were inferior to the white schools in terms of physical plant, teachers, and resources and a vigorous push to desegregate began. This desegregation push did not come without controversy. While there was not any particular formalized school segregation laws in Massachusetts segregation had become normative and even some African Americans disagreed with desegregation fearing it would result in African American students being forced to compete in the classroom with white children who had the cultural capital to outperform African American students. Ironically, as groups of African Americans first pushed for segregated schools in Boston, in 1846 we see groups of African Americans legally petitioning for desegregation in Massachusetts schools. Regardless of the conflicting views on desegregation the case of *Sarah Roberts vs. City of Boston* was brought before the Massachusetts Supreme Court in 1849 (Schultz 1973).

Sarah Roberts was a five-year-old African American girl who was forced to attend a segregated school. Sarah and her parents passed five white neighborhood schools on her long journey to the segregated, and inferior, black school. Her father held steadfast that this was ethically and legally unjust. Represented by Robert Morris and Charles Sumner, Sumner argued that there is only one appropriate type of school and that is one that serves all children. Unfortunately, the Supreme Court of Massachusetts ruled that the Boston school committee under Commonwealth law had the right to provide separate educational facilities to black pupils as well as to prohibit black students from attending white schools (Sumner 1849). The Negro School Abolition Society and Sarah's father continued the fight and in 1855 a law to end school segregation in Massachusetts was passed and schools were theoretically integrated that same year (Kendrick and Kendrick 2004). While this law was a precursor to *Brown v. Board of Education*, given the racial demographics and social structure, it did little to resolve the racial inequity in Massachusetts public schools.

THE ROLE OF TEACHERS

In addition to Mann's historic work around students, and various legal challenges to the Massachusetts educational system, in 1839, teachers, who previously held very limited credentials, now had the first state Normal School. The normal school housed in Lexington, Massachusetts, was specifically designed to train teachers. In the early years of the normal school, training was directed towards the early primary school years with secondary education training coming later. This education allowed for some uniformity amongst standards and expectations for teachers. Giving teachers in training a classroom laboratory of sorts and the ability to develop curriculum and teaching skills before entering a classroom, these normal schools allowed teachers to move beyond the rote memorization of the traditional classroom experience. Before this time teaching was not considered a profession, for without common teaching standards, anyone could teach. It should be noted, however, that most early normal school graduates only had acquired an elementary education themselves when entering the normal school where they would train for a year or two before returning to teach. The pay scale for teachers reflected the education levels; the paltry pay for untrained teachers was typically less than thirty dollars a month, elementary school normal trained teachers received more, and if one was a college graduate they tended to teach on the secondary level and received a higher salary (Ornstein, Levine, and Gutek 2010).

> Mann spoke at the dedication of the Lexington Normal School, stating "I believe Normal Schools to be a new instrumentality in the advancement of the race. I believe that, without them, Free Schools themselves would be shorn of their strength and their healing power and would at length become mere charity schools and thus die out in fact and in form." (Barnard 1851, 196)

In 1839, Mann expressed the strong sentiment that without the professionalization and proper teacher training, public schools would indeed die out or become vessels to house charity cases: in today's vernacular the poor, marginalized, the special needs students—indeed, the students with no other options. Mann's statement provides an ominous foreshadowing and warning for our current lawmakers and educational advocates.

THE FIRST HIGH SCHOOL

While schoolhouses became the norm in Worcester, the first high school was not built until 1845. Named the Classical and English High School, this school was located on Walnut Street. The first day opened for one-hundred and forty two students. Classes were held during the week and on Saturdays. In addition, in 1848 Worcester was chartered as a city with Levi Lincoln named the first mayor and Abraham Lincoln giving an address at city hall. The 1850s would bring the first national women's suffrage convention to Worcester and anti-slavery riots. Worcester was indeed a hub of educational and political activity (Rushford n.d.).

While Massachusetts had the Old Deluder Satan Act of 1647 and the Massachusetts Law of 1789, a true compulsory education law came into effect in Massachusetts in 1852, again the first in the nation. The 1852 law required that any person responsible for a child between the ages of eight and fourteen was required to make sure that child had at least twelve weeks of schooling per year with at least six weeks being consecutive. Failure to do so would result in a twenty dollar truancy fine. The school committee was responsible for enforcing this law. In 1873 the fourteen year old standard was reduced to twelve; however, the number of enrollment weeks was raised to twenty (Kotin and Aikman 1980).

Due largely in part to the compulsory education act and population increases by 1872, the seams of the Classical and English High were bursting with increased enrollment, and the school moved across the street to the corner of Maple and Walnut. This school was noted throughout the Commonwealth for both its academics and its architecture. The school held admission certificate privileges to all New England colleges and had a lengthy record of graduates awarded scholarships. The debating societies and athletic programs were also renowned. Within six years of building the first high school in 1851, coeducation between males and females on the secondary level was implemented in Worcester (Nutt 1919; Museum; League of Women Voters 1964).

Alternative education also began in the mid-1800s in the form of night school. In 1849–1850, the Worcester night school opened for adults who sought English language instruction. At the same time, an additional three evening programs were established, one female, one male, and one coeducational for traditional students. The night school curriculum was in line with traditional grammar schools, and, in later years, it progressed to the curriculum of the high schools. It was noted that elementary students were not successfully taught in the evening programs given developmental needs (Nutt 1919).

In 1857, Worcester's educational system implemented additional classes for students who were unable to excel in the traditional school setting. The reasons were listed as inability due to what was seen as parental neglect or basic misfortune. While segregated from traditional students, this was a first step in providing education for all children. In addition to these alternative programs, the Worcester School, a boy's trade school located in Armory Square, was established in 1909; it was the first of its kind in the state. The school admitted only boys or men over fourteen. It averaged four hundred day students and eight hundred men in night classes. Girls' trade soon followed in 1911, housed in an unoccupied wing of the boys' school. However, with a generous donation from David Fanning in 1917 the Girls' Trade School was built (Nutt 1919; League of Women Voters 1964).

During this time the population in Worcester was growing at an exponential rate. In 1873 the town would be described as "The Heart of the Commonwealth." It was noted that the central location of Worcester and the "intellectual vigor of its people" contributed to the rapid expansion of the town. The thirty-six miles of the city had 373 farms, 5,446 homes and 50,341 residents and 142 schools in 1873 (Nason 1873).

THE SCHOOL COMMITTEE

As noted, in 1823 Worcester became the first town in the nation to develop a school committee. The Worcester School Committee arose out of concern from citizens that the educational system was failing to do its duty. The committee comprised of men, set standards, regulations, and governed school development. The first woman joined the school committee in 1874, fifty-one years after the committee's inauguration. While a major milestone, women were only allowed to sit on the committee at that time; it took an additional six years for the first female school committee member to cast her vote in 1881 (League of Women Voters 1964).

The school committee held primary control of the educational system in Worcester and wielded tremendous authority as such. They instituted the minimum age of school entrance at age three, established codes of conduct and punishment, and enforced these regulations. For example, tardiness was considered a misdemeanor. Impertinence, obstinacy, neglect of duty, falsehood, obscenity, profanity, and quarreling were all considered crimes and punished as such. Student absences were only excused due to illness or if the child was out of town. If students violated any of these standards, teachers were charged with enforcing the consequences. Teachers were told to use a three-tiered approach to change the behavior. Persuasion, a discussion between student and teacher was the first stage. The second stage was admonition, a strong warning regarding the consequences, and the final stage was reproof, a formal consequence. If this failed to change the delinquent behavior, corporal punishment with the rod was normative and accepted. In addition to these regulations the school committee, in order to ensure the upkeep of the schoolhouses, mandated that any damage to the school would be paid for by the parent; the students also were responsible for cleaning the schools, including waxing and polishing desks and even sanding the floors several times a year (Daughters of the American Revolution 1903).

Worcester's school committee acted reasonably autonomously until 1905, when a group of concerned citizens banded together to form the Public Education Association. The Association expressed concerns that were twofold, the need to improve the quality of the connections between the community and the schools and the desire to maintain the highest educational standards for students. This Association, not the school committee, was pivotal in encouraging the commerce and trade school developments, pushing the need for school gymnasiums, and other matters of importance to the community. Indeed, the Association pushed strongly for hygiene and health to be part of the educational system, and in 1906, medical inspections began in the schools with the first school nurse appointment taking place in 1911 (Nutt 1919; League of Women Voters 1964).

In 1934 the school committee underwent one its most radical changes. It transformed from an appointed board into an elected school board, placing more power in the hands of the community and parents. The city voters would elect eleven members for a two-year term. In 1950 shifts in local government lead to a more streamlined committee of six elected members plus the mayor for a two-year term (League of Women Voters 1964). It should be noted that the role, power, function, and scope of the Worcester School Committee was not without controversy, and this controversy lingers today.

The nation as a whole underwent significant changes during the progressive era with a national income tax put in place and women gaining the right to vote. The economic prosperity of the era brought forth tremendous growth regarding the education of youth in Worcester. Elementary schoolhouses were normative with a nine year program of study. This would be reduced in 1911 to an eight year program. Five preparatory schools emerged for seventh, eighth, and ninth grade honor students. By 1954 only one, Woodland, remained. In 1892 kindergartens were also established. Also in 1892, a second high school, English High, located on the corner of Irving and Chatham

Streets, was built, pulling students from Classical and English High now known simply as Classical High (Nutt 1919).

EDUCATIONAL GROWTH

It was at the turn of the century in 1900 that we notice the emergence of the secondary schools that still exist in Worcester, Massachusetts, today. South High, located on Richards Street, entered the school department in 1900–1901. This school opened with four hundred students, however, within four years, enrollment rose to seven hundred and its peak of 1,025 students presented day to day challenges given the physical structure of the building. Temporary accommodations were utilized before an additional building could be constructed to meet the increased enrollment demands (Nutt 1919). South was seen as an exemplary educational model with 80 percent of its graduates going on to college and university studies. Again, South like Classical was noted for distinction, and in 1904, it graduated Robert Goddard, creator of the first liquid fueled rocket (Del Prete 2010).

North High came to be in 1911 and graduated its first class in 1913. The building was first housed on Salisbury Street, near the intersections of Grove, Lincoln, Belmont, and Main. North was first housed in a very dilapidated building. Noting the poor conditions, in 1916 a more modern building with auditoriums was built at the Salisbury Street site; the school housed 700 students. In addition to the extracurricular activities seen at the other high schools, North students also took part in the care of the Green Hill gardens.

In 1914 through development and reorganization, Classical High relocated to the site of the former English High, North stood at Salisbury Street, and South High remained on Richards Street. The former Principal of English High, Mr. Joseph Jackson, moved to the Walnut Street building and with the majority of teachers and students from English, opened the doors of Commerce High in the fall of 1914. Commerce housed on average fourteen hundred students and seventy teachers. It was the largest high school in Worcester and one of the largest in the state of Massachusetts (Nutt 1919).

Commerce was recognized as having a diverse curriculum, including business, banking, drawing, and journalism while still maintaining a rigorous academic curriculum as well. In addition to this tremendous growth on the secondary level, elementary schools in Worcester were now on an eight year schedule. The preparatory schools focused on college preparedness and introduced foreign languages, and the high schools were on a four year schedule (changed from the three-year cycle previous to 1911). Indeed, a town that appeared to be actively opposing education in its early development now appeared to be the flag bearer of public education in America, with the school district well deserving of recognition and the many accolades (Nutt 1919).

The post–World War I period brought attention to the school district's neglected middle school years. Junior highs did not even enter into Worcester's educational system until 1924 with the advent of Grafton Street Junior High. It was at this point that the district moved to a six-year elementary schedule and six-year secondary program, including junior high. With this development, we also see the first phase of school bus transportation beginning with junior high students living at least two miles away from the school. It was also during the 1920s that Worcester built twelve new schools and added thirteen additions to previously existing structures. The depression era of the 1930s brought a lull in physical plant development that extended into the 1950s, with only two schools built and one addition during these thirty years (League of Women Voters 1964).

While the physical plant was stagnated during the 1930–1950 time period several pivotal educational changes were taking place locally and nationally. In 1941 Worcester required all teachers to pass the National Teacher's Exam prior to employment. In 1947 a guidance program was developed and added to the school district's structure. Furthermore, in 1949 the Linn report established the need for twenty-two million dollars to be dedicated to improving the physical plant of the educational system in Worcester (League of Women Voters 1964).

Coming out of the depression and World War II era proved to be an exciting time period, for the 1950s and 1960s witnessed the Civil Rights Era. In Worcester, during the 1950s two additional junior highs were built, along with two more elementary schools and five building additions. The 1950s also brought merit promotions to teachers and subject specific department heads on the junior and senior high school level. Curriculum also experienced a massive shift with the introduction of tracking, or the grouping of students according to academic ability, at both the junior and senior high levels (League of Women Voters 1964).

MOVEMENTS AND CHANGES

As noted above, desegregation was a controversial issue during the civil rights era. The *Brown v. Board of Education* decision and several other pivotal acts and movements in the 1950s and 1960s would forever change the landscape of public education in Worcester and the nation as a whole.

Brown vs. Board of Education was a monumental legal case decided by the United States Supreme Court in May of 1954 declaring racial discrimination in public education unconstitutional and illegal. As noted above, the Massachusetts Supreme Court made a decision regarding desegregation nearly one hundred years earlier in 1855. It should be noted while the Supreme Court of Massachusetts ruled in favor of desegregation in 1855 it was not practiced in the majority of schools at that time. Given the ruling of *Brown v. Board of Education* the federal, state, and local governments were compelled to, in theory, desegregate schools because it was ruled separate was not equal. This ruling sparked hope for racial equity in the United States; however, it also resulted in various schools, agencies, and governments refusing to comply, hostility, racial violence, forced busing, and desegregation. While Massachusetts made legal history in 1855, in theory, the violence, hostility, and busing woes are well documented in this state as well. While seen as a landmark case, scholars argue that if the goal of *Brown v. Board of Education* was to provide integrated schools or equally funded schools, then the ruling failed miserably (Orfield, Frakenberg, and Garces 2008).

The Civil Rights Act of 1964 would also change the landscape of our nation and public school system. This Act was designed to eliminate various forms of discrimination. While *Brown v. Board of Education* spurred the racial desegregation debate, Title VI of this Act reinforced the desegregation of public schools across gender, ability, and language. An amendment to the Civil Rights Act was sparked by the National Organization of Women (NOW). NOW adopted a list of demands at the 1967 national conference that became known as the 1968 Women's Bill of Rights. One of the statements directly pertained to the role of females in education. "That the right of women to be educated to their full potential equally with men be secured by Federal and State legislation, eliminating all discrimination and segregation by sex, written and unwritten, at all levels of education including college, graduate and professional schools, loans and fellowships and Federal and State training programs, such as the job Corps" (Cullen-DuPont 2000, 332). This bill of rights thrust the women's rights movement into a national dialogue and sparked the 1972 amendment, Title IX, prohibiting gender inequity in education.

ESEA, or the Elementary and Secondary Education Act, was passed in 1965. This Act has proven to be one of the most controversial pieces of educational legislation in the history of the United States. This act emerged out of a need for all students regardless of race, religion, or gender to receive an appropriate education in order for all United States students to be globally competitive.

This act is largely viewed as the broadest, most sweeping education bill passed in the United States. Up until this point, public education was squarely a local and state governed entity. With the passage of this act, the federal government provided funds to well over 90 percent of public and parochial schools. Several titles under this act afforded school districts monetary resources. However, it also gave the federal government more authority in the function of public education, sparking controversy that continues to spur educational debates today.

Under this act, Title I monies are intended to support disadvantaged students, particularly special needs students. Title II provides money for library and audiovisual materials; Title III provides money to schools for at-risk students; Title IV provides money for higher education research on education; and Title V details the laws and provisions (Jennings 1995). It should be noted that this legislation has been reauthorized repeatedly. ESEA's present day incarnation is No Child Left Behind.

The 1968 Bilingual Education Act would emerge as Title VII of ESEA. This title established a policy on the federal level regarding the education of children with a limited English speaking ability. The title allowed for federal funds to be used to develop and implement programs for such children. This title has also been reauthorized numerous times over the past forty years. In August 2000 President Clinton signed Executive Order 13166 "Improving Access to Services for Persons with Limited English Proficiency" (Limited English Proficiency 2000).

BURNCOAT SENIOR HIGH SCHOOL

The 1960s also introduced the school at the center of this book. In 1964 Worcester established its first comprehensive high school, Burncoat Senior High School. In order to alleviate crowding issues at other Worcester elementary and secondary schools and to accommodate what was at the time the fastest growing section of the city, Burncoat Junior-Senior High School was built. This school served as the city's first junior-senior high combination school with a comprehensive curriculum.

Burncoat Junior-Senior High School offered a wide variety of courses at one location. It was the precursor to the curriculum now seen in all of Worcester public secondary schools with courses ranging from electives to college preparatory. Not only was Burncoat the first in the city to have outdoor athletic fields, it was also the first to be energy conscious, since two schools shared the same cafeterias and boilers. The plans for the junior high were approved in June of 1952. This construction eliminated grades seven and eight at Greendale, Adams, Harlow, and Burncoat Street schools, making more room for the increasing elementary school enrollment in the Burncoat neighborhood. Also, it allowed all students from Thorndyke Elementary who had been traveling to Grafton Street Junior High to now attend Burncoat Junior High. At this time, the preparatory school at Belmont Street closed, since those students would also attend Burncoat Junior High (Freid 1952).

Burncoat Senior High was slated to open in September 1964. The school was touted as the only secondary school in Worcester to offer both vocational courses, such as pre-nursing, industrial arts, and home economics, in conjunction with general education courses for those students who would be leaving high school at age sixteen to enter the workforce. The city also took great effort in planning the athletic facilities, providing space both in terms of land and in the curriculum for baseball, tennis, field hockey, football, and ice hockey for both boys and girls.

Built to house 1,500 students, the school's new construction and curriculum design had the longest school day for a high school in Worcester, 8 a.m. to 2:26 p.m. Students would attend seven forty-eight minute classes and have four minutes to pass between classes. On December 7, 1964, three months later than scheduled, Burncoat Senior High opened with 775 students, without a senior class (Burncoat high opens with 775 attending 1964). In 1969 Burncoat Senior High School received its accreditation and a ten-year membership to the New England Association of Colleges and Secondary Schools (Lynch 1969).

CONCLUSION

Settled in the 1600s and incorporated as a town in 1722, Worcester, Massachusetts, provides a rich case study in the development of an urban school district from the very beginnings of the United States of America. The roots of early American education are clearly anchored in the socialization of children and to the religious mores of the time. During the 1800s, reform movements pushed education towards an academically based curriculum in order to engender citizens who could contribute to the economy. While Worcester experienced some national firsts, such as the development of a school committee, Worcester's transition from home schools to fully accredited secondary schools exemplifies the trajectory that most urban school districts followed. Yet, the hurdles and subsequent solutions the Worcester School District faced from 1700–1965 were at times both unique and commonplace among developing school districts. Worcester's diverse population and rapid development will prove to present an entirely new set of challenges for the school system. Schools are communities and in order to understand the challenges faced by schools one must understand the larger community in which the school is housed.

AUTHOR'S NOTE

The stories of history, defiance in spending and educational support, and the painful history of segregation may seem less troubling as they appear—as antiquated tales of woe. However, the stories of the past creep into the present. Funding the districts plethora of schools remains a contentious battle every budget season. With recent reports in local magazines pinning the school committee against the state and city government with statements suggesting both entities are underfunding Worcester's schools in the hundreds of thousands to millions of dollars. Despite law that requires adequate funding, defiance, although often termed confusion presently, continues in Worcester. In Worcester, we need only look at the racial demographics of the 2011–2012 school system to determine if segregation persists. With the student population at 36.4 percent white and 63.6 percent minority, Flagg Street Elementary stands at 75.5 percent white, while two elementary schools only 1.5 and 1.8 miles away stand at only 8.9 percent and 6.1 percent white respectively. The middle schools in to which these elementary schools spill continue the disproportional trend with Forest Grove 45.6 percent and Sullivan Middle 28.7 percent white. There is a continuation in high school with Doherty at 46.35 percent white and South High at 24.6 percent. There is clearly a separation taking place. However, it is the result of a confluence of factors including race, socioeconomic status, and manmade quadrant lines that dictate which neighborhood feeds into which school. Why and where we send our children to school are personal decisions, yet the history of the Worcester Public School system is an inescapable ghostly presence in the lives of all connected to its present day incarnation.

Chapter 2

The Importance of Neighborhood

People on the outside don't understand we are more than just fights, they think we're so ghetto, it's so amazing on the inside. The bad neighborhood doesn't make bad people. I don't see it as a ghetto, it's a community.

—Sophia, eleventh grader at Burncoat Senior High

The known first usage of the term neighborhood was in the fifteenth century, articulating a section of land with individuals who possess similar characteristics. This brief definition does little to convey the importance of neighborhood. In simplistic terms neighborhood matters. As adults where one lives is often synonymous with who one is and what one has, it is frequently a source of pride or discomfort. When individuals choose a place to reside it is typically predicated on affordability, security, and more often than not the school system. A neighborhood can be a place of comfort, familiarity, and security or it can be the source of great emotional and sometimes physical discomfort. Children do not have a choice as to where they live yet the neighborhood in which they reside can have particular and often irreversible consequences for this vulnerable population. On average children who grow up in more affluent neighborhoods tend to have better outcomes as they grow into productive citizens.

"BETTER" NEIGHBORHOODS

Research has suggested several reasons for positive outcomes associated with affluent neighborhoods, these reasons also help to define what factors in combination create a better neighborhood. First, in better neighborhoods there appears to be more concern for the collective well-being, thus an increase in collective policing of the neighborhood. This collective social control has an impact on everything from lawn and home maintenance to an individual's behavior. Neighbors in better neighborhoods tend to be more involved and have higher expectations for behavior, thus resulting in a decrease in infractions ranging from disorderly conduct and vandalism to more severe and violent crimes (Ainsworth 2002). Social control in better neighborhoods can be seen in the formation of contractual neighborhood associations and the enforcement of agreed upon norms. However, often social control is handled in a less formal way through neighborhood gossip or day to day conversations between neighbors (Wilson and Taub 2006).

In addition, better neighborhoods typically have higher median household incomes as well as higher educational attainment amongst adults. These factors contribute to children having access to more resources including better schools, books, technology, healthcare, and extracurricular resources. Higher income and education also have a correlation with family stability, in particular parental well-being (McLoyd 1998). Being happier, less stressed parents with fewer financial woes allows for better parenting. The neighborhood also has an impact on children by providing a readily accessible peer group in which to connect with, children in better neighborhoods tend to have less access to troubled or deviant peers (Brody, et al. 2001). Parents organize play dates, construct friendships, and nurture neighborhood friendships outside of school in an attempt to socialize children with those from perceived like-minded families. This process contributes to the replication and reinforcement of neighborhood as well as family expectations and norms. Neighborhood matters significantly.

Just as better neighborhoods often have a positive impact on child development and later outcomes, a neighborhood in crisis can have a devastating impact on children. A 2009 report from the Urban Institute documents the myriad of challenges and consequences children in high poverty neighborhoods must contend with well before adulthood. The consequences are both mental and physical. Children living in high poverty neighborhoods have more cognitive delays, mental health disorders, and higher childhood obesity rates than those in more affluent neighborhoods. They are more likely to be involved in risky and delinquent behavior. Therefore as a consequence, teen pregnancy, adolescent arrests and incarceration, sexually transmitted disease, and school dropout rates are also significantly higher for children in these neighborhoods. The researchers at the Urban Institute note that these trends, while having a devastating impact on these children, ultimately impact the entire society as these children will grow into adults with substantially less earning power and more reliance on the government and tax payers for sustenance (Popkin, Acs, and Smith 2009).

THE CAPITAL GRAB

Neighborhoods also impact a child's social capital and occupational opportunities. Social capital can be defined as "the sum of the resources, actual or virtual, that accrue to an individual or a group by virtue of possessing a durable network of more or less institutionalized relationships of mutual acquaintance and recognition" (Bourdieu and Wacquant 1992, 119). Social capital can be simply viewed as the benefits associated with an individual's membership in a particular network. More specifically, when looking at neighborhood membership, children are exposed to role models, norms, values, and resources in their neighborhood. In better neighborhoods, in general, the norms and values that are modeled provide positive reinforcement for schooling, education, diligence, and perseverance as a route to economic success and happiness. In addition to role models, children in these neighborhoods often have access to networks of individuals that will assist them in educational and occupational endeavors, thus increasing social capital for these children. Children in more economically strained neighborhoods often see role models that are unemployed, sporadically employed, or underemployed in positions that are unfulfilling economically or otherwise. This limits these children's access to particular adult role models. Even more troubling is the long-term impact of chronic exposure to discrimination and oppression. Perceived or real, if children associate discrimination and oppression with a particular ethnicity or neighborhood population it can have a consequential impact on children's self-efficacy, motivation and goal setting. If children do not see formal education benefiting those around them, or those that look like them, they can develop an oppositional model to education and the American dream (Ogbu 1991). They may see other avenues to success and opportunity, both legal and illegal, as viable alternatives to formal education (Fisher 2005). Again, this is particularly true if they see no quantitative difference for those in their neighborhood who have successfully completed high school to those that had dropped out (Ainsworth 2002).

Beyond the individual, the community in which a school is located has a tremendous impact on the school itself (Grogan-Taylor and Woolley 2006). Neild and Balfanz (2006) also chronicle the impact of neighborhood on students and schools. The authors note that urban high school students have the highest dropout rates in America. In addition these comprehensive, urban, neighborhood schools have substantially higher numbers of minority, low-income, and special education student subgroups yet receive significantly lower funding and fewer resources than their suburban counterparts.

The location of a school in a particular neighborhood also can impact a school district's ability to attract and retain the best teachers. This can have a ripple effect on the atmosphere of the school, student behavior, and time on learning. In addition, the location of a school in a particular neighborhood can impact enrollment significantly, with families petitioning the district for permission to transfer into or out of a particular school. These school choice students take their funding with them leaving the urban school with less financial resources to educate the remaining students. In some cases parents are so desperate they lie about residence to avoid sending their children to schools in particular neighborhoods.

> On January 26, 2011, ABC News reported the case of an Ohio mother who was jailed for sending her children to a non-neighborhood school by lying about her address (even though the children's father lived in the more affluent neighborhood). The district fined Kelley Williams-Bolar thirty thousand dollars and when she refused to pay she was convicted, served ten days, and received three years' probation. Ms. Williams-Bolar stated she lied because her neighborhood and school were unsafe. (ABC News 2011)

Almost every state has cases such as Ms. Williams-Bolar wherein districts and schools that are in demand are using private investigators, surveillance, and interrogation to weed out the non-neighborhood interlopers. Parents are being fined and arrested and students are being plucked out of classrooms and sent back to their often inferior and sometimes dangerous neighborhood schools. This trend has sparked outrage from both sides of the fence. Community members from the more disadvantaged neighborhoods question the moral, ethical, and legal grounds which allow the city, state, and federal government to force children into inferior schools, while children blocks or miles away receive a quantitatively better educational experience. The feeling for these parents, regardless of ethnicity, is separate, not equal. On the other side, community members from the preferred districts and schools point to their higher tax burden and contributions, as well as voluntary parent donations as key to the status of their high quality schools and feel it is an earned right. The American concept of capitalism certainly impacts the concepts of earned rights and privileges. If one ascribes to the earned right, meritocracy philosophy, anything can be attained through hard work, and if a parent wants a child to attend a particular school that parent should work hard to live in the neighborhood, in order to attend said school. The right to live in a particular neighborhood speaks to one of the fundamental traits of American culture, individualism. Based on this ideal it is an individual's hard work that affords them the right to live in a better neighborhood. If an individual fails, therefore, the consequence can then be squarely placed upon their shoulders, and in the case of education their children's shoulders. Thus, by holding true to American individualism society and those living in the more affluent neighborhoods owe nothing to those that have not and are therefore waived from any moral or fiscal responsibility. Indeed, neighborhood matters emphatically.

THE TALE OF TWO BURNCOATS

So what then is the Burncoat neighborhood? Tree lined streets, quaint colonial homes, brick and steel housing projects, police cruisers, little league fields, the sounds of children laughing and the ice cream truck passing, this is the Burncoat neighborhood. Bound by West Boylston Street, East Mountain Street, Lincoln and Burncoat Streets, the rapid development of what is now known as the Burncoat neighborhood spurred the building of Burncoat Senior High. Neighborhoods have collective histories and Burncoat is no different. In order to understand how Burncoat Senior High came to be we must first understand the neighborhood in which it sits and the population the high school serves. The history of the Burncoat neighborhood, like most urban neighborhoods is complex. This chapter gives some insight into how this American neighborhood came to fruition.

Historically, two major residential developments took place in the 1900s that would bring this neighborhood to life; the 1922 development of what was known, in the developmental stages, as Bedford Heights and the 1950s development of the Curtis Apartments and Great Brook Valley Gardens. During the 1700s and much of the 1800s what is now known as the Burncoat neighborhood was agriculturally based land much like the rest of Worcester, large plots of farmland owned by a handful of wealthy residents. From 1898 to 1911 there was a move towards subdividing the larger farms into smaller plots of residentially owned land. However, at this time the land was still by in large agriculturally based. It is also during this time in 1896 that the first hospital was built in the Burncoat neighborhood, indicative of the growing population (Nutt 1919). With the changing industrialized economy, in 1922 city maps show a push for greater development with areas of the Burncoat neighborhood marked for future development. This proposal and development came to be known as Bedford Heights.

Bedford Heights is the neighborhood bound by Clark, Quinapoxet, Longmeadow Streets, and St. Nicholas Ave. The farmland that made up this area was subdivided into small plots of land for individual homes. What was once one farm in 1911 became plots for dozens of homes by the early 1930s. These plots were purchased by individual families and thus began the extensive population of the Burncoat neighborhood. As decades passed the Bedford Heights section of Worcester became home to many of Worcester's middle class families of Irish and Swedish heritage. The neighborhood was known for housing many of the city's teachers and policemen, as well as workers from the nearby Norton Company. Families took great pride in the beautiful colonial homes, tree lined streets, and the sense of community that the Burncoat neighborhood afforded its residents. In fact as the decades passed it continued to be a very desirable location to own a home in Worcester as it afforded homeowners a sense of community and of suburbia in the city with easy access to highways as they were developed.

Very little has been written on this neighborhood. However, in the 1990s the *Worcester Telegram and Gazette* reported some minor incidents of teenage drinking and vandalism in the neighborhood prompting a call for a curfew for adolescents; however, this call was quickly quieted and no curfew came to be (Kotsopoulos 1997). Overall, the Burncoat neighborhood remained a much desired, predominantly white, middle class, family neighborhood until recent years when an uninvited invader would change the landscape of the community.

The Asian Longhorn Beetle would infest the trees of the Burncoat neighborhood prompting the United States Department of Agriculture to cut down thousands of trees on both city and privately owned property with thousands more slated for removal and even more slated to be injected with a toxin to eradicate the beetle. This infestation combined with the economic recession caused a dramatic reduction in home values and consumer demand for homes in the Burncoat neighborhood. What was once a neighborhood coveted for its idyllic setting and tree lined streets now resembles the urban city that the neighborhood is a part of with more asphalt and concrete than trees and flowers (Dayal 2009). That being said, one could still walk the Burncoat neighborhood and find generations of families whose children and grandchildren attended Burncoat High School, indeed families who would not ever call any other Worcester neighborhood home.

In addition to the Bedford Heights project, the second contributing factor to the rapid rise of the Burncoat population was the development of the Curtis Apartments and Great Brook Valley Gardens housing development. In 1951 the state of Massachusetts funded the building of 390 low-income apartments for returning World War II veterans known as the Curtis Apartment Complex. A year later Great Brook Valley Gardens was funded by the federal government with six hundred apartments. The buildings were steel framed, reinforced concrete, and faced with brick, the project was made up of five streets: Constitution Ave, Tacoma Street, Freedom Way, Chino Ave, and New Vista Lane.

This federally subsidized complex consisted of ninety-one separate buildings: sixty one-bedroom apartments; 302 two-bedroom apartments; 202 three-bedroom apartments; thirty with four-bedrooms, and six with five-bedrooms. The Worcester tornado of 1953 that killed ninety people also severely damaged both the Great Brook Valley Gardens complex and the

Curtis Apartments, however both were rebuilt. In 1955, the Great Brook Valley Gardens complex had a population of five hundred men, 594 women, and 1,650 children. The complex's population much like the city of Worcester's population was overwhelmingly white. The rent in 1955 was $20–$56 a month and occupants enjoyed amenities such as laundry, dry cleaning, and bakeries. Tenants waxed poetically of the "excellent view and cooling breezes in summer" and tenants were said to keep their apartments "shining with care" (Sandrof 1955). Residents enjoyed the location as it was "close enough to the city—and yet you're far enough away so that you're almost in the country" (Sandrof 1955).

The tenants of the complex were carefully screened and hand selected by a selection committee which formed in 1946. By 1955 the selection committee had screened over ten thousand cases and selected twenty-eight hundred families based on income and fit, resulting in a complex comprised of elderly (downsizers), returning veterans, and families. The committee then interviewed each family once a year to determine if they still met eligibility requirements. The turnover rate was approximately 20 percent a year. The Curtis Apartments and Great Brook Valley Gardens provided a much needed low-income rental alternative for the residents of Worcester and in the 1950s through the early 1960s appeared to be a textbook success story (Sandrof 1955).

By 1965 the publicized image of a successful housing project began to fracture. In 1967, what was a simmering problem within the community became a very public issue. The population of the project fractured into two opposing populations; the veteran and elderly residents versus the increasing numbers of young families. These tensions spilled into the newspaper. What was once seen as the joyful frolicking of youth throughout the complex only ten years early began to erode; complaints of noisiness, disrespect, and of destructive unsupervised youth were common (Rent-Subsidy Program is Favored 1967).

The tensions and hostility that were rising to the surface also had some racial undertones, as it was also during this time that the project began the shift from a predominantly white tenant population to that which included more African American and Latino residents (McHugh 1960). As the 1970s approached there were both great strides and great turmoil in the housing complex. In 1971 and 1972, respectively, Great Brook Valley Gardens witnessed the opening of a child care center and a health center. In 1978 the Great Brook Valley Health Center would be expanded. As the project sits on the edge of the Worcester city line, residents previously did not have easy access to child care or medical facilities. The child care center afforded many of the residents an opportunity to garner employment with the assurance that their children would be in a safe friendly environment close to home.

In addition, the medical center gave residents easy and affordable access to both preventative routine care, as well as sick visits. Given the location of the complex and income level of its residents, the development of the Great Brook Valley Medical Center and its subsequent expansions would have, and continues to have, a profound impact on the health and well-being of the residents of the complex and of the citizens of Worcester as a whole (Duckett 1995). These developments in the 1970s improved the quality of life for many of the projects low income residents.

RACE RIOTS AND CRISIS

As noted the 1950s Great Brook Valley Gardens and the Curtis Apartment complexes were painted in a utopian light, while the late 1960s saw tensions between residents primarily based on age. The 1970s and 1980s would see the project enter a period of racial violence that had been festering for some time. The images of sparkling floors and tranquil breezes were replaced with images of unhappiness and unrest. As racial tensions increased so did the white flight from the complex. The housing authority that had seen ten thousand applicants for twenty-eight hundred spots would see 10 percent of what were then 869 units empty by 1974 (McGrath seeks funds to police housing projects 1975). The project also lost the word Gardens from its public identity and was now known as the Great Brook Valley Housing Project or simply Great Brook Valley, and in common vernacular "the valley." While this may seem a slight change the word garden signifies home, peace, tranquility, community, and suburbia to many. Thus, the removal of this word is a subtle change that was indicative of the changes Great Brook Valley was experiencing.

In July of 1975 racial tensions hit a new high when one hundred to 150 individuals were involved in a gang fight along racial lines between African Americans and whites. Using bats, chains, and hockey sticks the riot raged on, frightening and angering many of the hopeless residents. Residents implored the Worcester Housing Authority security force to keep the complex safe. Feeling the pressure from the community and the Worcester Housing Authority administration the Great Brook Valley security force began to crack down on gang activity and other violent incidents. More patrols were successful at keeping some of the criminal activity at bay and the numbers of arrests increased, offering at least some modicum of reassurance for the worried residents (Blunt Jr., GBV Disturbance Injures 1; 3 Held 1975).

This would appear to be a marked improvement, however, many residents accused the security force of acting with bias and brutality against the minority residents of the complex. The perception of the largely minority housing

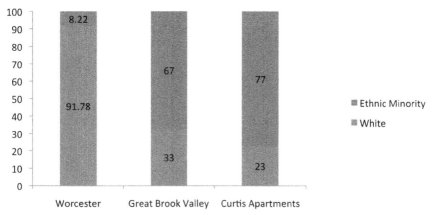

Figure 2.1   1980 Racial Demographics.

project was that the Worcester Housing Authority security force was seen as solely acting in the best interest of the white residents (Bushnell 1979). In 1979, four years after this incident, the racial pendulum had swung and tensions now were predominantly between the white residents and Latino residents of the project. With upwards of four thousand residents at any given time two thousand of the residents were Puerto Rican. The Latino residents felt extremely unsupported by the Worcester Housing Authority. Miguel Rivera, a Latino activist, warned ". . . if things don't change in GBV innocent people could lose their lives" (Tension Reported High "Incident Feared" at GBV 1979). Unbeknownst to Mr. Rivera his words would ring loudly and true, an ugly and violent wake-up call was about to hit the Worcester Housing Authority and the city.

In 1979 and 1980 the Worcester population was 91.78 percent white, with 4.25 percent of Spanish origin, 2.76 percent black, and 1.2 percent of other ethnic origins (Collier 1986). Great Brook Valley and the Curtis Apartments did not reflect these statistics (see Figure 2.1), with the projects by 1979 being 67 and 73 percent minority and at least two thousand of the four thousand residents Latino (Bushnell 1979). While the numbers of Latino residents continued to rise, their voices and numbers were not reflected in the staff of the Worcester Housing Authority or resident housing association, which remained white. Thus, the Latino residents were the majority in numerical terms, however, they still remained the minority in terms of power. The feelings of racial oppression and the tensions that had been simmering would lead to an explosion of violence in May of 1979.

On May 28, 1979 the streets of Great Brook Valley would erupt in a large fight between several youth and the Worcester Housing Authority police. These larger fights and riots were becoming more commonplace as the tensions in the

Valley were getting more and more difficult to contain. This particular incident required the Worcester Housing Authority police force to call in thirty Worcester police officers and fifteen state troopers as back up in order to break up the disturbance. It was estimated by police that over 300 individuals were involved in the melee and the initial confrontation was sparked by the perceived harassment of Latino residents by the Worcester Housing Authority police force. While the violent riot included hundreds it would only result in the arrest of two Puerto Rican brothers (Blunt Jr. 1979). Although only the two were arrested these arrests again ratcheted up the racial tensions in the project.

As summer bore down on the concrete and brick complex, the residents warned of an impending disaster (Bliss 1979). The housing officials refused to feed into the hysteria opting instead to downplay recent events. The day after the riot several adults witnessed a Worcester Housing Authority police officer passing young Puerto Rican children and shouting swears at them as they played outside. This officer would later be identified as Hiram Estremera. In a cruel twist of fate Officer Estremera was one of two affirmative action officers hired by the Worcester Housing Authority force in response to the constant criticisms of the Latino residents. In order to quell the criticisms related to the lack of diversity on the Worcester Housing Authority security force, Estremera was hired in 1978. Almost twenty years old, a high school drop-out, with no experience, and no psychological evaluation Mr. Estemera patrolled the volatile project. Mr. Estremera showed no affinity for the Latino residents and his hire did little to reassure the residents. As the summer of 1979 approached, tensions remained high and residents became increasingly uneasy.

In early June 1979, a meeting was held between community leaders, the Worcester Housing Authority and project residents to discuss the police brutality and racism at the Great Brook Valley and Curtis Apartments. Emotions ran high as complaints and documentation of the racial harassment and the perceived injustice Latinos were experiencing in the complex were put forth. The housing authority and police offered up their own poll that showed the residents of Great Brook Valley were happy with police and security (Bliss 1979). The Latino residents took what appeared to them to be a fabricated poll as an act of further degradation (Bliss 1979). In addition, the Latino residents expressed fear and anger regarding a related issue that they believed extended beyond the project. Many of the Latino residents believed strongly that as their population was growing in Worcester there was a concerted effort by the Worcester Housing Authority and the city leaders to segregate them and the entire project from the rest of the city. As Miguel Rivera, director of the Latin Association for Progress and Action, said, "the project's isolation separates it from the city as surely as apartheid separates blacks from whites in South Africa" (Lewis 1979). As the Latino residents of the project saw strength in their numbers and pushed for more rights and control in the project, the Worcester Housing Authority and its police force pushed back with equal force. The racial tensions in Great Brook Valley could no longer be harnessed after a horrific scene unfolded in June of 1979.

Officers Hiram Estremera and Angel Rosario were on patrol at Great Brook Valley on the evening of June 20, 1979. At approximately 12:30 a.m. (June 21, 1979) the officers noticed a car leaving the housing project with a stove in the trunk. They followed, believing the stove may have been stolen from the project. The officers stopped the car and found two men inside. Officer Estremera proceeded to ask the driver, Angel Luis Allende, for his identification which was promptly supplied to the officer. At this point Estremera recognized Allende as an individual whom he had stopped in the past for motor vehicle violations and who he had felt had given him a "rough time" during those stops. Estremera's partner, Angel Rosario, asked Mr. Allende where the stove had come from and Allende explained that his sister had given it to him. At that juncture, Estremera felt an arrest was imminent and he radioed for back-up.

Worcester Housing Authority Officer Ferraro arrived on the scene inciting anger from Mr. Allende who then became belligerent and accused the officers of harassment. Mr. Allende's belligerence turned to violence and he punched Officer Ferraro. Ferraro arrested Mr. Allende for assault and battery and handcuffed his hands behind his back. Estremera patted him down. A small knife was found on his person. While he was being placed into the back of Estremera's cruiser, Allende continued to shout and make serious threats, largely in Spanish which both Officers Estremera and Rosario spoke and understood. Mr. Allende told the officers that they would be sorry because this harassment and arrest would result in a riot in the project, that he would burn down the project, and that he would ultimately kill the officers (*Commonwealth vs. Hiram Estremera* 1981). What appeared to be the idle threats of an angry man, some of Mr. Allende's words came true in the forthcoming hours.

After Mr. Allende was secured in the back of Estremera's cruiser, the officers started their short journey back to the Worcester Housing Authority police station. Officer Rosario was driving Allende's car with the other male passenger still inside, Estremera was driving his cruiser with Allende handcuffed in the back seat, and Ferraro followed in his cruiser. After driving only about 100 feet, a gunshot was heard by Officer Ferraro. Estremera pulled over, Ferraro followed. Ferraro looked on in horror as Estremera pulled Allende's lifeless, handcuffed body out of the back seat. Allende had been shot pointblank in the face and killed. (*Commonwealth vs. Hiram Estremera*, 1981)

As word spread throughout the project about the killing of an unarmed, handcuffed man, violence erupted that raged on for days. Property destruction escalated and fury abounded. The Worcester Housing Authority Police Station within the complex was fire bombed. The Worcester Housing Authority force, unable to regain control, requested back up from other law

enforcement agencies and over 250 police and riot teams patrolled the housing project. During this riot, thirteen people were arrested and an additional
thirteen were injured (Lewis 1979).

At trial, Estremera's defense team would claim mental illness partially due
to the constant violence and riots in the project. In fact, immediately after the
murder, Officer Estremera was inconsolable and claimed to not remember
the shooting. His defense team would claim Officer Estremera was put in an
untenable position as a Latino officer in Great Brook Valley and that he had
been threatened numerous times. They would argue that the racial unrest as
well as the culture of fear and violence in Great Brook Valley compounded
Officer Estremera's mental illness. However, given the evidence presented,
in the end Mr. Estremera was convicted of second degree murder. During the
sentencing the Worcester Housing Authority would also have their moment
of judgment. While the Worcester Housing Authority was not on trial, the
judge in the Estremera case criticized the Authority for their negligence in
knowingly hiring a nineteen-year-old with no experience, nor having conducted a true background check or psychological evaluation (*Commonwealth
vs. Hiram Estremera* 1981).

In 1980, with the majority of the Curtis Apartments and Great Brook
Valley's 4,500 person population now Latino, violence and racial problems
persisted. With a population that was 62 percent Hispanic, 24 percent white,
and 14 percent black, and a median income of $8,425, struggles for power
and voice within the project continued to be a salient theme among residents. The racial imbalance within the project led to desegregation proposals
that would evict many minority families to bring the project to a fifty-fifty
majority/minority population (Bliss 1979). In an effort to gain representation,
the Latino population at Great Brook Valley rallied for control of the 1981
Tenants Association Board. Thirty-two were nominated and for the first time
in the history of Great Brook Valley the association would be run by Latinos
(R. R. Bliss 1981).

In addition to the Tenants Association Board victory, the Latino residents
would also gain another long fought victory. After continuous debates and
numerous complaints ultimately three years after the shooting of Allende, the
ten member Great Brook Valley/Worcester Housing Authority security force
was eliminated and security was put into the hands of the Worcester Police
Department (Kotsopoulos 1982). While seen as a victory by many residents,
this switch did little to improve the violence and gang riddled conditions of
the project. In 1984, mail service to the Curtis Apartments was halted after an
assault on a female letter carrier, the fifth assault on letter carriers in a year.
As assaults, gang violence, and drug activity increased; there were reports
of police and fire departments not responding to emergency calls in the Valley. There is some documentation upholding such charges. During the 1980s

Great Brook Valley and the Curtis Apartments experienced hundreds of nuisance dumpster fires a year. Calls for help came so often that the fire department instituted a "no response" policy to dumpster fires (Della Valle 1989, Monahan 1988). By the end of the 1980s, the federal and local government acknowledged the housing project was plagued with criminal activity and responsible for over 40 percent of all drug activity in the city of Worcester. Many believed this to be a low estimate (Della Valle 1990). The desegregation proposals did not come to fruition in Great Brook Valley and the Curtis Apartments. Thus by 1988, the two projects were 70 percent and 76 percent minority (Collier 1988). The end of the 1980s would also bring in Jordan Levy as mayor of Worcester. Mayor Levy was committed to improving conditions in Worcester, including Great Brook Valley. Mayor Levy would also play an important role in education reform in Massachusetts that will be discussed in chapter 3.

A CALL FOR CALM AND ZERO TOLERANCE

The 1990s emerged with the replication and magnification of the same issues of the 1980s. Now the project was largely minority in population. The summer of 1990 saw similar riots of the past. In July 1990 as school was out and the sun bore down on a simmering population a riot involving over four hundred people exploded onto the asphalt streets of Great Brook Valley. The fighting in what was deemed by authorities as a "string of battles" brought over fifty police officers to the Valley. In the end nine adults and seven juveniles were arrested, with three officers injured and six cruisers damaged (Griffin 1990). The saga continued when individuals attempting to bail out those who had been arrested erupted into a fight at police headquarters. Six more would be arrested (Griffin 1990). A common and all too familiar theme emerged with news coverage once again pitting police against residents. Charges of racism and undue police force were leveled against the Worcester Police Department (Doolan 1990). Emotions and rhetoric became so intense that on July 26, 1990 the United States Justice Department announced that a representative would attend an upcoming meeting over resident-police issues (Hammel 1990).

After the 1990 meetings residents were again reassured that the city, state, and federal government were committed to racial equality and promoting better resident-police relationships. While different government agencies were verbally committed to changing the culture of Great Brook Valley very little changed. Three years later, in 1993, a drive-by shooting would rock the community. Following the shooting yet another riot would spew onto the projects streets. This riot would involve over 150 young people setting fire to numerous cars and even attacking a television crew's van (McFarlane 1993; Shaw 1993). This year would also bring about the election of Worcester mayor, Raymond (Ray) Mariano.

Mayor Mariano had an affinity for Great Brook Valley. Raised by an immigrant mother and veteran father he grew up in Great Brook Valley. Upon his election Mayor Mariano wasted little time expressing his commitment to cleaning up the Valley. Indeed, 1993 would be a turning point for Great Brook Valley, during this same year police would identify three major gangs as running the project and its violent drug trafficking ring, federal agencies joined the city in an attempt to eradicate the project of the gang activity (McFarlane 1993).

As the 1990s continued, the fight to clean up the Valley and improve the quality of life for residents became a full blown battle (Williamson 1990). Some light was seen as a larger more comprehensive health center opened as did a gym and installation of playground equipment for the complexes children (Astell 1998). As the twenty-first century dawned upon the city of Worcester, Great Brook Valley and the Curtis Apartments underwent an extensive rehab to add greenery and alter the exterior of the buildings. In addition to the Worcester Police, private security also patroled the properties. The Worcester Housing Authority, with now former city mayor Raymond Mariano as its executive director, also adopted a zero tolerance policy on drugs with aggressive enforcement and eviction policies if drugs are found in any apartments. However, the project and its residents still struggle to shed the image of a violent, unsafe environment. The reputation and stigma lingers.

THE MICROSYSTEM

The history of the Burncoat neighborhood, particularly that of the Bedford Heights development and the Great Brook Valley and Curtis Apartment projects present the backdrop for what will be Burncoat Senior High School. As noted, this one neighborhood which will be the feeder for the high school is made up of two very distinct populations and sub-neighborhoods within a larger neighborhood context. The students at Burncoat Senior High will emerge from the quiet colonial homes and perfectly manicured lawns as well as the steel, concrete and brick housing projects. They will emerge from the historically middle class community largely of Swedish and Irish heritage and from the largely Latino low-income housing project. They will emerge with images, stereotypes, and bias absorbed from the elaborated tales discussed across the dinner table or on the streets, or heard by eavesdropping on adult conversations. They will emerge from their microsystems with various levels of social capital.

The microsystem, according to psychologist Brofenbrenner, is our inner world, our neighborhood, our family, our friends, and our school. As such our microsystem has a profound impact on our socioemotional development. Therefore, any racism, violence, prejudices one is exposed to repetitively in this system will have a quantitative impact on who that child will come to be, conversely any positive, trusting, nurturing relationships will also be impactful. The connections between those groups within our microsystem are referred to as our mesosystem. For example, how parents and schools communicate with each other will also impact the child. If families do not trust the school or teachers, or the school staff has a certain perception and relationship with the neighborhood residents this too will impact the child. The above mentioned relationships have proven to have a direct impact on student achievement (Brofenbrenner and Morris 2006).

CONCLUSION

The tensions that permeate the microsystems from which Burncoat students emerge will prove to have a great and long lasting impact on the evolution of Burncoat High School. Built in 1964, Burncoat Senior High is less than fifty years old, however, the institution's memory predates the physical structure. Historically, the past fifty years has brought tremendous shifts in the economy, racial demographics, and the educational system of the United States. Neighborhood matters and this neighborhood's, Burncoat and Great Brook Valley, history is wrought with specific incidents that magnified the discrimination, oppression, and struggles for change that were happening across the nation. Understanding the community in which Burncoat was formed and the students that emerged from this community is pivotal as we look at Burncoat Senior High School today.

AUTHOR'S NOTE

Most parents would agree that we want our children to grow up in a good neighborhood. What is up for debate I suppose is what makes a good neighborhood? Expansive yards that afford luxury homes and offer the opportunity of a passing wave to neighbors from a distance and scheduled activities at which adults may socialize while the children frolic or huddle on the most recent technological devices; the sounds of crickets more common than the sounds of sirens, is this the neighborhood you dreamed of? A city landscape where nightly conversations take place on the front steps to socialize and escape the oppressive heat, while children play with a hose, or hydrant water and the sounds of sirens become white noise as you catch up with friends new and old, is this your neighborhood? Each experience shapes us as social beings, provides us with capital, helps to determine how we see the world and interact with our fellow citizens as we venture outside of our neighborhoods.

Chapter 3

A Portrait of an Urban High School

The mind is not like a vessel that needs to be filled, but rather like wood that needs to be lighted.

—Plutarch, Plutarch on Education: Embracing the Three Treatises (CW Bardeen, 1910)

Home of the Patriots, Burncoat Senior High School, located in Worcester, Massachusetts, is a mid-sized urban comprehensive high school comprised of students grades nine through twelve. Worcester's educational system is divided into four geographically based quadrants and Burncoat Senior High School services students in the Burncoat quadrant. The students of Burncoat Senior High emerge from ten local elementary schools and merge into Burncoat Middle school which is physically connected to Burncoat Senior High.

Before further discussion of Burncoat Senior High it should be noted that much of the data discussed in this chapter and the following chapters was collected through two rounds of surveys administered to all ninth, tenth, and eleventh grade students. The survey utilized was the High School Survey of Student Engagement in 2008 and 2009. The survey was quantitative by design but allowed for open ended responses as well. In addition, focus groups were conducted with students during those same years and again in 2011. Interviews were also conducted with the principal of Burncoat Senior High as well as the superintendent of the Worcester Public Schools.

During the 2010–2011 academic year Burncoat Senior High School had a population of 1,072 students. By race the school student population was 40 percent white compared to 68 percent across the state's student population; 34.8 percent Hispanic compared to 15.4 percent statewide; 18.7 percent African American compared to 8.2 percent statewide; 4.9 percent Asian, 1.3 percent multi-race, and 0.3 percent Native American (see Figure 3.1).

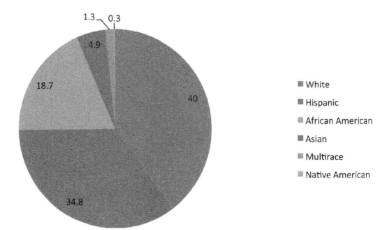

Figure 3.1   Burncoat 2011 Demographics.

By gender the school had 505 male students and 568 female students. By numbers alone Burncoat Senior High is a minority majority urban school (Massachusetts Department of Elementary and Secondary Education 2011).

For 38 percent of students at Burncoat, English is not their first language compared to 43 percent district-wide and 16 percent statewide. In addition, 17 percent of Burncoat students have limited English proficiency (LEP) compared to 32 percent in district and 7 percent in state. Fifty-nine percent of Burncoat students are classified as low-income compared to 32 percent district-wide and 7 percent statewide. Burncoat has 22 percent of its students receiving some form of special education compared to 21 percent district-wide and 17 percent statewide. These statistics indicate that the majority of students at Burncoat may require some form of remedial assistance whether in English language development or special education.

The Massachusetts Department of Elementary and Secondary Education (DESE) also calculate mobility rates in schools. Mobility rates document the number of students transferring into or out of public schools. Burncoat's mobility rate was 13 percent overall. However, for the Latino, limited English proficiency, and special education subgroups the percentage of transferring students rose to 20 percent per subgroup. While the white student population only saw an 8 percent mobility rate (Massachusetts Department of Elementay and Secondary Education 2011).

MOBILITY, DROP-OUTS, AND PUNISHMENT

The discussion of mobility is an important one as it has a direct correlation with academic achievement. Student mobility is linked to higher retention levels and failure to graduate. It is clear that students that have a propensity to transfer between schools both within and outside of school districts lose time on learning by missing academic content along with days in school. Mobility also impacts continuity of learning which in turn impacts achievement. However, there are also social factors that are impacted by mobility and these too have an impact on academic achievement. In his article entitled, "Toward Understanding How Social Capital Mediates the Impact of Mobility on Mexican American Achievement," Robert Ream discusses the importance of understanding mobility, social capital, and achievement amongst the Latino population. As the Latino student population in the United States continues to mount at an exponential rate, the achievement gap between Latinos and white students stubbornly persists. Ream argues that mobility impacts achievement by impacting Latino students' social capital. By limiting the time students, especially adolescent students, have in a school to form a social network and build trusting relationships, social capital is negatively impacted (Ream 2005). As teachers attempt to educate an increasingly diverse population the quest becomes even more challenging as mobility rates rise. Mobility rates shift with economic downturns, therefore, one could predict mobility rates to increase in coming years especially in urban school districts amongst the least economically stable.

During the 2009–2010 academic year Burncoat had what appears to be a relatively low and normative 5 percent drop-out rate compared to a nearly 4 percent district rate and 3 percent state rate. However, if we examine the 2010 cohort of 327 students the drop-out rate rises significantly. Of the 327 students 17 percent dropped out, compared to 12 percent district-wide and 8 percent statewide. The numbers are even more troubling for some student subgroups at Burncoat. Again looking at the 2010 cohort; 35 percent of limited English proficient students; 28 percent of special education; 25 percent of Latino; and 20 percent of low-income students dropped-out of Burncoat Senior High (Massachusetts Department of Elementary and Secondary Education 2011). Thus, the overall dropout rate can be deceiving. Even more troubling, the engagement survey conducted at Burncoat during this same academic year indicated 16 percent of incoming ninth graders had already considered dropping out. One year later the ninth through eleventh grades saw that number who considered dropping out surge to 31 percent. Of that 31 percent, 50 percent stated the teachers were the reason behind their desire to drop-out of Burncoat. Some went as far as to state that teachers at Burncoat Senior High had encouraged them to drop-out.

Burncoat's 2010–2011 data also exhibits high percentages of deviant behaviors and punishments within the school. In-school suspension rates were at 16 percent, nearly double that of the 9 percent district-wide and four times the 4 percent statewide average. Out of school suspensions rose to 17 percent compared to 13 percent district-wide and Burncoat's numbers were three times the 6 percent statewide rate (Massachusetts Department of Elementary and Secondary Education 2011). Although, the administration is working diligently to reinforce school policy only 55 percent of Burncoat's students reported feeling safe at school according to the engagement survey. Only 53 percent believe the school is applying rules and punishments in a fair and consistent manner. Yet, some students, particularly the seniors are quick to note that "there has been a lot of improvement since my freshman year with violence because of Mr. Foley's leadership." Principal Foley also notes that while it is difficult to shed the image of an unsafe school:

> There has been a significant drop in four years in regard to fighting. I do believe that the community is coming to recognize that this is a safe school and children who come here are safe. Then they can look at what we have to offer them educationally. I don't think it has anything to do with diversity. It doesn't impede us or make the school any less safe. We have a similar set of expectations and the manner in which we apply those expectations are very consistent. An indicator of safety and of school climate of the four major comprehensive high schools our suspension rate is significantly lower. We had about 500 issues of suspension in one year (1000–1200 students). There are other schools that have twice as much. The bulk of our suspensions are with the same 200 students.

While suspension rates are troubling the truancy rate was even more astounding at 36 percent compared to a district rate of 28 percent and state rate of only 2 percent. By the end of the eleventh grade 47 percent of Burncoat's students acknowledged they had skipped school. Given this data it is not surprising to see Burncoat's retention rate at over 9 percent, double that of the district's 3.6 percent and over four times the state average of 2 percent (Massachusetts Department of Elementary and Secondary Education 2011).

Remarkably, even with the drop out, suspension, and retention rates Burncoat saw a 66 percent graduation rate for the 2010 cohort compared to a district average of 71 percent and state average of 82 percent. The number rose significantly for certain subgroups at Burncoat. Asian students had an 80 percent graduation rate, African American students had a 73 percent rate, and white students had a 70 percent graduation rate. While this data is hopeful, the numbers also reflected a steep drop in graduation rates for other student subgroups. Only 59 percent of low-income students from this cohort graduated, as did 53 percent of Latino students, and 48 percent of special education and limited English proficient students respectively (Massachusetts Department of Elementary and Secondary Education 2011).

In 2010–2011, Burncoat had eighty-four teachers to meet the needs of these 1,072 students. This would reflect a 13:1 student teacher ratio if classes were equally divided. However, they are not, so many classes burst at the seams with twenty-five to thirty students per teacher. The staff at Burncoat is not ethnically reflective of the student population. Of the entire staff twelve are ethnic minorities while 118 are white; comparatively, the student population is over 60 percent minority.

As an urban school, in an urban school district, Burncoat Senior High has faced cuts to programs and extracurricular expenditures due to budgetary constraints. As one student acknowledged, "Teachers try hard, funding is the biggest problem." While this student is correct, funding is a problem; thanks in large part to committed staff on the district and school level students at Burncoat still have the opportunity to participate in many extracurricular activities. Athletic teams include cross country, track, field hockey, football, soccer, volleyball, basketball, tennis, baseball, and softball. In addition, students can participate in some district wide sports including crew, lacrosse, golf, swim, ice hockey, and wrestling. The offerings at Burncoat extend beyond athletics as students participate in a variety of afterschool clubs and service organizations including the International Club, JROTC, the Math Club, Best Buddies, the school newspaper, the Student Council, the National Honor Society, and the National Spanish Honor Society. Indeed, Burncoat Senior High School offers many opportunities for its students to develop academically, physically, and socially. The extracurricular activities serve to create community within the halls of Burncoat. There are great opportunities for students to bond with one another as well as faculty. However, many students report that only a small fraction of students participate, those students are the high achievers. Unfortunately even with these opportunities, only 40 percent of students would choose to attend Burncoat Senior High if given a choice according to the student engagement survey. While many reasons for this statistic emerged, the first relates to academics.

ACADEMICS

During their academic career students at Burncoat are placed into several different academic tracks based on ability: special education, bilingual/English language learners, college preparatory, honors, and advanced placement (AP). Advanced juniors and seniors can also participate in dual-enrollment at local colleges and universities. The roots of ability grouping, also known as tracking, are evident as early as the 1892 National Education Association's Committee of Ten recommendations for a varied curriculum in order to meet the needs of the increasingly diverse American school population.

These early forms of tracking were used to Americanize immigrants and segregate African Americans as well as to educate children into their appropriate class or role in society. It was clear during the foundational years of tracking that children's placements were based on subjective analysis as well as their race and class (Bowles and Gintis 1976). Ability tracking was and is still a controversial topic in Worcester as it was implemented during an era of desegregation and is often seen as an institutional tool utilized by school systems to continue segregation and institutionalized racism. In a 2009 article, Ansalone notes that numerous research studies indicate a link between a student's class, race, and educational placement. This data reveals that students from lower socioeconomic groups as well as blacks and Latinos are disproportionately placed in lower track classes. This placement often occurs without any supportive evidence for the placement. Rather placement is based on evidence such as anecdotal teacher recommendations. Ansalone also notes that the majority of research finds that tracking does little to promote achievement; rather it impedes equal education opportunities on both the local and national levels. Studies suggest that tracking can be a self-fulfilling prophecy. When students are placed into groups based on subjective measures often their own expectations and the teachers' expectations become aligned with the stated level of the group and thus students do not rise past that expectation.

Advocates of ability tracking view it as a necessary educational tool that allows schools to provide various levels of instruction to an academically diverse population. Advocates also view tracking as a tool schools can use to ensure high ability students are challenged and low ability students are not lost, since tracking allows teachers to be more specific with instruction. Regardless of the perceived benefits, researchers such as Jeannie Oakes (2005) have documented the negative impact and constitutional challenges tracking presents. The ultimate consequence of tracking is that it reinforces racial and class inequity systemized through public education; thus, what should serve as the key to success, a student's education, becomes a method of sustained marginalization. The impact on Burncoat Senior High students supports the large body of research on tracking.

"School is separated by academic level. There is diversity in my honors and AP courses but college prep? Mostly minority and they just don't care. They're not as motivated." Maxine's statement is troubling as it not only speaks to the ethnic segregation taking place between the tracks but also the internalization and reinforcement of stereotypes by students. Keran echoed Maxine's statement "We're so separated, the college prep kids do nothing and don't want to be involved." Some of the students were more positive in support of ability grouping. Anthony offered "I learned a lot here and there are definitely higher expectations in honors and AP." Lena also added, "Trying to learn in the college prep classes, you have to fight through the noise. Honors is a gift, a real gift. You learn you can focus in silence."

However, the positive spin also reflects a different level of expectations and relationships between those students in various ability groupings and the staff of the school. No group feels the impact more than the college prep/ regular education students. This student population had the highest rate of disengagement at Burncoat. The majority of college prep students reported that they did not care about Burncoat, on the whole they did not feel safe, and certainly they did not feel good about the school. In addition they also reported feeling as though their teachers did not believe they could produce excellent work nor did they believe the teachers wanted them to do their best. Students outside of the college prep track acknowledged that college prep at Burncoat fails to prepare students for college. They questioned the legitimacy of the courses and the intent of the staff as well.

The school district's numbers pertaining to tracking in 2010 reflect the Burncoat students concerns. While white students made up 36 percent of the Worcester public school student population they took 48 percent of advanced placement seats, 46 percent of honors seats, and 35 percent of college prep seats. The black student population in the Worcester public schools was nearly 14 percent in 2010, these students took a proportional number 14 percent of advanced placement seats, 15 percent of honors, and nearly 16 percent of college prep seats. However, the Latino population saw the biggest inconsistencies in ability placement. While making up nearly 39 percent of the Worcester public school student body they only took 18 percent of advanced placement seats and 24 percent of honors seats. However, they populated 41 percent of the college prep seats (see Figure 3.2) (The Commission for Latino Educational Excellence 2011). What these statistics show

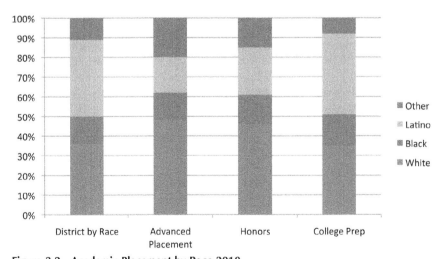

Figure 3.2   Academic Placement by Race 2010.

is that while black students appear to have a relatively normative placement in courses white students are disproportionately placed in the higher tracks while Latino students are disproportionately placed in the lowest academic track. Given the changing demographics of the United States, this district is but one snapshot of the larger picture being referred to as the "Latino education crisis" by many educators (Gandara and Contreras 2009).

Historically, in Massachusetts, college prep courses were considered general education. That is, until it was discovered that general education courses were not only failing to prepare students for college, these courses were also failing to provide students with a rigorous education. So Massachusetts had a solution. A solution that would impact Worcester's school system as Superintendent Boone notes:

> When the solution to bringing rigor to education was to take general study courses and give them the label of college prep it was probably the worst thing . . . the worse thing this Commonwealth could have done and allowed. Effectively what they did was create a joke system because every student who wants to go to college knows that you don't want to be in any course that carries the title college prep. What we did was basterdize these courses. And so what we did, the state did, this is my home now, so I say we, what we effectively did was put another label on something. Not kicking Brown because Brown was phenomenal, we wouldn't be having this discussion today if not for Brown but the next part to Brown is what we're dealing with now. All we simply did was avoid a lawsuit. But we never changed expectations and it took me eight months here fulltime before we realized what college prep courses were and I'm still in shock over that. And so that's part of the Massachusetts context. . . . We may have put college on the general studies courses, but that's all we did. It's still overrepresented by low income students, students of color, and students with disabilities so we put a new label on it and kept doing the same things. . . . The state has to own some of the direction districts have gone in. From my perspective if the students are able to compete, paying attention to the current and future work force then I have to start that in pre–k. We're trying to build into the pipeline going into science in the middle school we're doing new labs, redoing high school labs in order to make sure our students have what they need for AP. One of the other things I've learned in Worcester is that we were saying we had a lab period but it was really just on paper. Where we have gaps we have huge gaps. We are trying to address the whole piece . . . of really building college and career readiness it's about shifting the mindset. I'm astonished at the classes we have, we've taken some courses off line—such as Head Injury English and Head Injury Math curriculum this was on the books. We were defining classes by the needs of the students. You know I said eleventh grade English is eleventh grade English. What we may have to do is provide accommodations for some of the students to access and excel in the class. But it's one class eleventh grade English. We enhanced the rigor through honors level courses; hopefully, it's

still one of my biggest concerns. The AP is still the same. This is where I push back; there are those that want to say there is greater diversity in AP so it's not valid. Every student should have the opportunity to be successful. Historically in this country private schools emerged after integration as a means to continue to sort and separate, so did gifted education whether we want to own it or not. Now that students who normally wouldn't be in some of these classes are there there's the next push. We have to integrate within the walls.

In addition to the traditional forms of academic ability grouping, Burncoat Senior High School has another grouping that clearly delineates and defines students both socially and academically. Burncoat Middle and Senior High schools are home to the Worcester Public Schools Fine Arts Magnet Program (Evaluation Gives High Rating to Burncoat Magnet Program 1986). This magnet program takes an art centered approach to education that in these economic times is in stark contrast to what is normative in most urban public schools. Students at Burncoat Senior High in the Arts Magnet are afforded an opportunity to hone their craft as they participate in college preparatory courses in music, dance, theatre, or visual arts. This magnet program is home to some of the state's most talented adolescent musicians, dancers, and actors. Their performances and productions rival those of any performing arts school. This magnet has created a community; one might say a small school, within the larger school context of Burncoat Senior High. As Maxine stated "The magnets help so much, it makes Burncoat what it is. It's your safe place, you're accepted, it's a family, and I'm not going to be judged." The impact of this bifurcation of the student body is based on one's perception. Many students within the magnet program stated that the magnet makes Burncoat special, and that they and their parents chose Burncoat Senior High because of the magnet. Those students looking into the magnet from the outside voiced frustration that the magnet students truly believe magnet students are exceptional and better than the general population at the school. Students of color voiced concerns that the magnet appeared to be a place for white students and the students of color in the magnet were not your average students of color at Burncoat, just mere tokens. Perception or reality, the existence of the magnet serves as yet another tool to separate the student body at Burncoat Senior High. Historically, and justifiably, a source of pride for the district, the impact of the existence of this magnet on students is mixed at best.

POLICY VS. PRACTICE

Burncoat's educational policies as well as its successes and failures, and the opportunities it affords its students are all mitigated by state and federal educational policy. As documented in chapter 1, Massachusetts has played a significant role as a leader in educational advancements. Before the discussion of No Child Left Behind (NCLB), acknowledgment of one pivotal act that would impact the state educational system and consequently Burncoat Senior High is imperative. The 1993 Massachusetts Education Reform Act would be an extensive piece of legislation that would transform the landscape of public schooling in Massachusetts.

After two years of revisions and concessions with the goals of accountability, common standards, and higher achievement, the 1993 Massachusetts Education Reform Act (MERA) came to fruition. As stated in the previous chapter Mayor Jordan Levy took office in 1988. He wasted little time in joining others in a lawsuit to remedy the inadequate funding and unequal education provided to students in different Massachusetts urban school districts. Mayor Levy's, as well as a 1978 case, were rolled into *McDuffy v. Secretary of the Executive Office of Education.* Mayor Levy's intent was first an acknowledgment that the Commonwealth had failed its duty to provide an equitable education based on the Massachusetts constitution and then for the state to remedy the situation. Unlike Worcester's town leaders of the 1600s and 1700s, Mayor Levy would actually put the city in position to demand more educational resources from the state rather than the city skirting Commonwealth law. What the court would partially conclude in this case is:

> What emerges also is that the Commonwealth has a duty to provide an education for all its children, rich and poor. . . . Additionally, the record shows clearly that, while the present statutory and financial schemes purport to provide equal educational opportunity in the public schools for every child, rich or poor, the reality is that children in the less affluent communities (or in the less affluent parts of them) are not receiving their constitutional entitlement. . . . The bleak portrait of the plaintiffs' schools and those they typify . . . leads us to conclude that the Commonwealth has failed to fulfill its obligation. (*McDuffy v. Secretary of the Executive Office of Education* 1993)

The court issued its decision on McDuffy and the state responded several days later with MERA. The nuances of the reform law were controversial in 1993 and remain a bone of contention across the state. In Worcester, one can witness the impact of the 1993 reform act through the discussions at Worcester's weekly school committee meetings, union negotiations, or by simply observing in a school.

> The state and national context around education will always be there it always has been. We have folks that complain about requirements. Let's go back to ESEA, title 1, chapter 1, there has always been requirements. We got to a point with greater inclusion. Massachusetts as a state is dealing with and really responding and reacting to a history that has perpetuated some of this. When

we think about all of the leading national roles that Massachusetts has played in education, to Deval Patrick and Paul Reville's credit they are very clear in saying we have a huge achievement gap. But we suffer from a great deal of pride, "but we are first in this." Part of the public education story still gets hidden behind the "buts" at the end of the sentence. If you look at the decisions that came after the 1993 Ed reform act, which was very progress thinking, the challenge that occurred in Massachusetts, sometimes, local control and local involvement, we all know constitutionally there is a great deal that talks about states' rights as it comes to education. So even though folks think it's totally locally controlled, particularly in a community like Worcester where two-thirds of our foundation funding comes from the state. We can't ignore the state role in education. (Superintendent Boone)

THE POWER GRAB

As stated, the goals of MERA are commendable, however, in order to meet these commendable goals the state of Massachusetts took on many challenges that are considered "third rails" in educational circles including: funding, unions, testing, and power. No Child Left Behind did not emerge until 2001, therefore, Massachusetts, through MERA, was once again a leader in educational reform and thus educational controversy.

Funding was a key component of MERA and one that directly impacted Worcester. Recognizing the disproportionate funding of school systems within the state based on local funding contributions MERA sought to level the funding playing field. Therefore, the state, through MERA, adopted a policy of level foundation funding in order to mitigate the differences in education funding between lower socioeconomic districts and those that are more affluent (Massachusetts Department of Elementary and Secondary Education 1993). Unfortunately, this level funding policy does not come without controversy. Part of this legislation requires the school district to keep allocating local funds in order to meet level funding in combination with state monies. There was also to be a foundation budget setting that was to be reviewed every five years in order to ensure an appropriate budget per student given inflation, which has not come to fruition. Given the difficult economy of the early twenty-first century, towns and cities such as Worcester were stretching every penny with various stakeholders vying for every cent in the budget. In Worcester, this places the city government in the unfortunate and uncomfortable position of competing with the city school department for funds. City politicians and residents are often outraged at the amount of money being dedicated to the school system while other public services are cut including those services that have a direct impact on the health and safety of residents. The rhetoric includes accusations of a bloated educational system and misuse of funds. However, what complicates these arguments are federal and state law, much of which came out of MERA and NCLB. Due to these legislative acts funding must be kept level in Worcester according to the standard set by the state. Unfortunately, the state base line for the foundational budget has not kept pace with inflation or with rising health care costs, leaving the city school system to reallocate funds. In addition, the foundational budget is a basic, bare bones approach to educating children. Worcester's government and residents have adopted a policy of only funding the education of students at this foundational level set by law. While the school committee and superintendent would like to see this low financial bar raised, much resistance is met and funding remains dictated by MERA.

MERA also took on teacher unions in 1993. MERA sought to eliminate tenure for teachers. The language of MERA allows for the principal to remove "tenured" teachers with the approval of the superintendent for "inefficiency, incompetency, incapacity, conduct unbecoming a teacher . . . or insubordination." While this technically eliminated the role of tenure in Massachusetts schools, the wording in contracts, appeals process, and recourse available to unionized teachers did not allow for true implementation of this provision. In addition to this provision, principals were removed from the collective bargaining unit under MERA allowing for more autonomy in the principal position. Principals would gain the autonomy to run the school without being beholden to the union; however, it once again sets the stage for mistrust and a power battle between administrators and teachers. MERA, while granting this autonomy also sought to encourage participation from the parents and community, thus requiring SITE councils at every school, comprised of parents, teachers, and the school principal in order to aid in school based decision making (Massachusetts Department of Elementary and Secondary Education 1993).

In addition, Massachusetts adopted state mandated testing through MERA as a way to measure achievement based on the established curriculum guidelines. The Massachusetts Comprehensive Assessment System (MCAS) was the assessment tool of choice and will be discussed later in this chapter. The goal of MCAS was to provide a level of accountability and ultimately improve student achievement across the state.

MERA continued to address the lines of authority by attempting to give more control of the schools to superintendents along with the principals, removing some of the power from the strong hold of the local school committees (Massachusetts Department of Elementary and Secondary Education 1993). However, the language in MERA allows for a continuation of stressed power relations and awkward dynamics. While the superintendent is charged with the day to day operation of the school system the school committee still retains the power to hire and terminate the superintendent, review and approve the school budget, and contribute to educational goals and policies. After the 2009 Worcester elections it became apparent that the school committee of 2010–2012 was bifurcated along the lines of those that supported the superintendent's hiring, educational and professional competency, and autonomy and those that wished to retain the school committee power reflected prior to the 1993 act. This power struggle would prove to have unintended consequences for the educational system of Worcester and bring race back to the forefront.

Dr. Melinda Boone has been on one side of this power struggle in Worcester. Dr. Boone is the first female and African American superintendent the Worcester public schools have hired. Her 2008 hiring and subsequent contract renewal shed an uncomfortable spotlight on much that has been discussed regarding the history of Worcester in the first several chapters. Dr. Boone is seen as the best thing that could have happened to the school department and city by many as she was named the 2011 Person of the Year by the *Worcester Magazine*. Others view Dr. Boone as an interloper. By these constituents she is seen as someone who does not have the best interest of all students at heart. Rather, Dr. Boone's community engagement and attempts at bringing all constituents to the table for conversations regarding education has been perceived as a bias in favor of ethnic minorities and the low income population of Worcester. The fear is that Dr. Boone's administration is leaving the white middle-class students to blow in the wind. However, regardless of constituents personal feelings the data shows Dr. Boone is making improvements based on educational policy and the best interest of the school district in trying economic and political times. Although her contract was renewed for another three-year term the issues of race, equity, and justice for the community that her contract negotiations brought forth remained salient and contentious issues.

The public spectacle that played out in the school committee sessions and local newspaper during the fall of 2011 served to only inflame and reinforce the painful past and present that many ethnic minorities in Worcester experience. Unfortunately, the treatment of Dr. Boone was an example of disrespect that resonated with the ethnically diverse Worcester population. Even more unfortunate is that it was tied to an all-white school committee thus engendering and reinforcing distrust between elected educational officials and the community for which they were elected to serve. As stated, this distrust between parents and superintendent, community and school committee, will have an impact on the students in the Worcester public schools, and Burncoat Senior High is no exception.

NO CHILD LEFT BEHIND

While Burncoat Senior High felt the shifts of MERA, much like the entirety of public school districts in the United States it has felt the tremendous impact of the legislation known as No Child Left Behind. As noted in chapter 1 the Elementary and Secondary Education act emerged in 1965. In 2001 it was reauthorized as the No Child Left Behind Act. Enacted as "An Act to close the achievement gap with accountability, flexibility, and choice, so that no child is left behind," No Child Left Behind has become an unwieldy piece of bureaucratic legislation that many would argue has ushered in an unprecedented wave of rigid testing and punitive measures that has lessened flexibility, choice, and creative thinking in the classroom. This act has tied the hands of school districts, principals, and teachers. The act states that all children will be proficient in core subject areas by 2014. This statement or mandate alone is statistically impossible. From a scientific base we know that all children have innate cognitive potential that can be nourished through education, however all children are cognitively unique. With variation in cognitive potential, intrinsic and extrinsic motivations and attributions, to continue to ascribe to the belief that all children will be academically proficient in English Language Arts and Mathematics by 2014 is a belief that flies in the face of reality and doomed this Act from its inception. In addition, given the economic downturn during the era of No Child Left Behind school districts are left with budget gaps in the millions, their states running gaps in the billions and a federal government trillions of dollars in debt. This fiscal crisis has left districts with limited financial resources to achieve this idealistic and impossible mandate (U.S. Department of Education 2001).

The four basic tenents of No Child Left Behind are accountability, more freedom for states, implementing proven successful educational methodologies and more choice for parents. On face value all of these tenents appear positive and in the best interest of students. However, when we look at the practical implementation of these tenents we get a much different view. Accountability is the one tenent NCLB has been successful in implementing (U.S. Department of Education 2001).

What was once a benign word has now been tainted to the extent that one could argue it should be referred to only as the "A" word. How do districts show they are accountable? Districts show they are accountable through testing, testing, and more testing. Districts then report the results to the state and federal governments. For example, according to the Worcester Public Schools website every school in Worcester must have an instructional focus.

Burncoat's instructional focus reads as such:

At Burncoat High School, all students will experience a rigor based curriculum taught through instructional strategies meant to improve reading comprehension as measured by MAP, MCAS, PSAT, SAT, MEPA, and AP scores as well as other formative assessment.

Burncoat clearly is relying heavily on standardized test assessment in order to document reading improvement in order to meet the accountability mandate (Worcester Public Schools 2011). Each state decides what testing measure it will use to assess students. This is yet another fundamental flaw in the No Child Left Behind legislation. The inequity in academic rigor between state assessments not only leaves gaps amongst the students in the state but huge gaps between entire states. Massachusetts is revered as the standard for comprehensive high stakes testing utilizing the Massachusetts Comprehensive Assessment System (MCAS) to evaluate student performance in grades three to ten. Students are compelled to take these examinations across disciplines in order to meet NCLB standards as well as to graduate from high school. As more students pass the MCAS the state alters the test to make it more challenging. The MCAS and assessments such as these are referred to as high stakes examinations because they have severe consequences for students. For example if MCAS is not passed but a student meets all other requirements, the student will not receive a diploma rather they will receive a certificate of completion which is fundamentally useless for college admissions, and most employment. No longer are report cards and teacher ascribed grades the gold standard for how much a student has mastered, rather a plethora of standardized tests have become the benchmarking tool of choice.

CHOICE AND CONSEQUENCE

Whose choice one may legitimately ask. If we start from the student and work outward we can examine the impact of this "choice." Students in Massachusetts are subjected to several days of standardized testing over the course of a 180 day school year. Countless weeks are spent preparing the students for these examinations, homework assignments and class time is spent learning how to correctly answer the types of questions they are going to encounter on the exam. Students recognize the importance of MCAS with teachers and principals expressing the seriousness of the tests and dire consequences should students not perform well. Students are told you mustn't be sick or absent, messages are left for parents stressing the importance of early bedtimes, proper nutrition, keeping the students happy and positive, all as to not have a negative impact on the students test performance. During those weeks of testing in the Fall and Spring the impact is felt school-wide with the need for more silence, reduced volunteers in the schools, reduction in "specials" such as library, gym, art, music, even recess. These subjects are considered "specials" because due to budget constraints and time on learning requirements many schools have eradicated these programs. The results vary from anxious to apathetic students; obviously high stakes testing would not be the choice of children. One student articulated the feelings of many students in his response to the question of how to improve Burncoat "No more standardized tests please!"

The teachers also feel the direct impact of No Child Left Behind. Autonomy has been taken away from the classroom teacher. Now, with the pressure of testing bearing down the propensity to teach to the test is prevalent. In education we know this is not best practice however with the stakes so high what is a teacher to do? The NCLB mandate would allow a school district that has an underperforming school to fire or relocate the majority of the teachers within the school. In addition the current U.S. Department of Education administration is discussing the possibility of student performance based pay for classroom teachers making the situation dire. The result of high stakes on teachers and the possibility of salary or raises tied to students' performance will undoubtedly leave our most high need students without qualified teachers. Teachers must now attempt to teach in a way that is standardized, yet differentiates instruction for the diverse inclusive classroom population, all while their employment hangs in the balance. Teachers question the fairness of identifying schools as underperforming when there are a myriad of factors that contribute to learning that have very little to do with the education teachers are providing. In addition, teachers are often lacking the resources needed to teach, such as updated, or even enough books. Once a school is identified as in need of improvement staff morale often drops substantially, and once intervention takes place feelings of disrespect and distrust set in (McQuillan and Salomon-Fernandez 2008). Indeed, the requirements of NCLB have served to alienate teachers and fracture relationships within schools and across districts, amongst administration and staff. Surely, these high stakes tests and subsequent consequences would not be the choice of teachers.

Parents and families also experience the impact of No Child Left Behind. The anxious and apathetic students described above must be supported by families who in many instances do not understand the tests or have ambivalent feelings about the tests at best. After testing parents must decipher the results and deal with the consequences on their child, their school, and the district. Elementary school parents worry if the scores will impact middle school tracking, middle school parents worry about high school tracking, and high school parents agonize about graduation. When speaking to parents not one conversation ends without parents recalling their own educational experiences when more intellectual freedom was allowed and intellectual curiosity was nurtured. Art, gym, music, even social studies and civics are seen as additives or specials when they were once an integral part of the educational experience. NCLB and MCAS have changed the landscape of curriculum in schools across Massachusetts.

> Massachusetts followed NCLB and allowed funding to dictate what they were going to focus on so when you look at MCAS it's been ELA and Math. Some other states Virginia, pre-NCLB focus on the 4 core now we know that AYP (adequate yearly progress) and all that with NCLB have certainly raised math and reading and it is a foundation and we certainly need to think about that but there's shock if you will across the commonwealth, that our students who graduate high school aren't prepared for entry level positions in STEM (science, technology, education, math). Through self-reporting on the SAT only about 25 percent of high school graduates indicate that they intend to pursue a STEM major. The state has not had a focus on elementary and middle school science. (Superintendent Boone)

Parents question what will become of their students after their senior year when life does not provide a bubble sheet to fill out. When children are faced with questions and problems that do not have one direct answer that was previously fed to them what will happen to these students? Unfortunately, parents, much like the students and educators, recognize that the decision to become a testing American school system was one made by politicians who have often never attended a public school and most likely have not been educators. We only need look to the elite private and parochial elementary and secondary schools in the Unites States for some guidance as it pertain to these high stakes tests. Most do not require these tests for promotion or graduation. Higher education has also begun to realize the limitations of judging students based on an individual test score. In fact, many elite institutions have either done away with the SAT requirement or have declared the scores optional for admission. The question then remains why is the American k–12 education system fully entrenched in this testing structure?

According to No Child Left Behind Legislation and requirements, Burncoat Senior High School has failed to meet adequate yearly progress (AYP) for three years and they are now a level 3 school. In 2010 the data shows that only the white student subgroup at Burncoat Senior High met the performance target in English Language Arts and Mathematics while the minority, low income, and special education subgroups failed to make AYP in either academic grouping. As a level 3 (out of 4) school Burncoat High is eligible for intensive assistance from the state and federal government to turn the school around. When a school reaches level four status a complete and radical restructuring takes place. This can include closing the school, removing the principal and 50 percent of the teaching staff, turning the school over to a private organization to run, or restructuring. Restructuring would require the removal of the principal along with curriculum changes. Worcester recently had two elementary schools in this situation requiring the removal of the principals and curriculum changes. A third Worcester elementary school Burncoat Street, a Burncoat Senior High feeder school was also placed at a level four status in 2011.

Massachusetts has been involved with interventions on the local education level well before NCLB. In 1988, Massachusetts allowed Boston University to control the Chelsea Public schools when that district was deemed underperforming. In 2004 the state declared all schools in Holyoke and Winchendon underperforming and intervened. Unfortunately, state boards of education were not designed to handle the level of intervention required by NCLB. In their report, McQuillan and Salomon-Fernandez examined the role of state intervention required by NCLB. It is clear that states are at a disadvantage when it comes to the expertise or ability to turn around low performing schools. The authors also note that the majority of schools needing intervention are urban, and have large numbers of low-income and non-English speaking students adding to the complexity of providing a knowledgeable and adequate intervention.

According to the Burncoat Senior High School Accountability Plan, the administration at Burncoat is well aware of the strengths and areas of concerns regarding NCLB and student performance. The data presented in this plan, from 2008–2010, indicated that 78 percent of tenth graders who had taken the MCAS in eighth grade showed improvement in tenth grade. Unfortunately, it is also noted that the English language learner population is not performing as well, consistently performing lower than district and state averages. In addition, while the students as a whole are improving upon their eighth grade placement, Burncoat's MCAS results fall significantly below state averages. From 2002–2010, Burncoat Senior High tenth graders performed, on average, 18 percent lower in English Language Arts (ELA) and 22 percent lower in Math in comparison to state averages during this time frame. However, one may ask how does the Burncoat staff deal with these consequential statistics?

We've got a lot of people on the staff who were students at Burncoat and who come back. Certainly, you know as far as how do we handle being identified as a school in need of improvement? We think about it as a school that is improving. We're working on continuous improvement and continually improving instruction, working on relationships with grade nine and ten kids. We focus on MCAS we'd be foolish if we didn't. We offer tutoring after school, intensive service during the school day as well. We do those things because it's a big deal, for us and the kid too. The kid has to pass. The pressure exists. It is different for the staff who graduated in the 1960s, 1980s, and 1990s its generational (feelings about the student body). But I think we all understand what we need to do. I think we haven't had a lot of attrition (teaching staff at Burncoat), generally people that can't make it, don't have the skill set (to teach) leave. Some people change districts and go outside the district; they may have succumbed to the pressure. My teaching staff is stressed by the level of parenting that the kids have not got and that they feel they have to give. (Principal Foley)

The combustible combination of overreliance on standardized testing and accountability being utilized as a punitive weapon has altered the landscape of Worcester's public schools and that of many of our nation's schools in scope and function. In Worcester, one can walk down any particular hallway in any particular school and see test scores on display. In the elementary schools this may come in the shape of a rocket or horses racing with numbers on their backs. While no names are present children stand by and acknowledge that their horse is almost at the finish line while others lag by the entry gate. As the students get older the data appears as clear numbers a low range, mid-range, and high range and stickers are placed to acknowledge where a student falls. Consequently, these numbers then feed into student academic placement on the elementary level. While no formal system of tracking is acknowledged at this level informal tracking has typically commenced by the end of third grade in most school districts. This is normally seen through reading groups in the early elementary years. While data has shown that homogenous grouping tends to show benefits for high ability and gifted students the benefits for low ability and average students tend to be minimal at best. In addition questions as to the impact of tracking on self-esteem and the inflexibility in movement between tracks once a student is identified and labeled is of great concern to many (Allan 1991). In fact, some researchers argue that by the end of third grade we can for the most part identify how a student will be placed in high school. Thus, the trajectory begins very early and the impact of ability grouping, testing, and NCLB has and will continue to have dire consequences for many of our nation's children. In 2012, President Obama and his Secretary of Education, Arne Duncan, began the process of granting NCLB waivers to states. However, the waivers are designed to give states more autonomy in dealing with underperforming schools; the waiver does not absolve states of their testing requirements. In addition, opponents of the waivers suggest it will once again make the plight of the oppressed and marginalized invisible, resulting in throwaway students. Massachusetts will most likely adopt the PARCC (Partnership for Assessment of Readiness for College and Careers) as an MCAS replacement to better align with the new

Common Core requirements in the upcoming years. Thus, Massachusetts students will continue the standardized test battle.

CONCLUSION

Much like Worcester is an archetypal American city, Burncoat Senior High is a portrait of an American urban high school. The diversity of Burncoat's population is reflected in the ethnic heritage, socioeconomic status, and ability levels of the students that learn within its concrete walls. Many high stake decisions that impact our current American educational system and ultimately Burncoat are made at a bureaucratic level far removed from the classroom. While decisions are made purportedly based on the best interests of students much gets lost in translation from Washington, DC, to the classrooms in every American town and city. While education policy has been enacted purportedly in the best interest of children the policies discussed in this chapter: tracking, magnets, MERA, and NCLB have had the intentional and often unintentional consequences of segregation, separation, and alienation. These consequences do not discriminate and have impacted administrators, teachers, school boards, families, and ultimately the students. For six years I conducted various projects with and in Burncoat Senior High: focus groups, interviews, observations and surveys of student engagement. Researchers, lawmakers, and educators believe we have the answers or at the very least are attempting to find the answers that will fix what ails our urban educational system. However, students do not have to attempt to find evidence or answers. From a very early age children can and will clearly and concisely articulate the differences and disparity they witness and experience in their everyday lives. To listen to students, to listen to children, is often the gift of brutal honesty. The next two chapters give voice to the experts, the students at Burncoat Senior High, and a view into students' perceptions and feelings regarding their urban education experience in America.

AUTHOR'S NOTE

The test does not tell the whole story. I tested well, my oldest tests well. Last year my daughter was invited to apply to a "gifted and talented" program at another local public middle school based on her MCAS scores. The premise of this selective public program is that these children will be in an academically challenging environment and be provided with many enrichment opportunities both academically and culturally. I did not have her apply. In addition, the looming question is why can't her neighborhood school provide the same enrichment opportunities? The memories of being the only minority in most of my honors and advanced placement classes linger. The stories of the Burncoat students resonate. As Dr. Boone states all students deserve an opportunity to be successful. Learning in peace should not be a gift rather it should be an expectation. Access to cultural resources, the arts and enrichment classes should not be based on self-selection, luck, race, or income rather they should be accessible to all. Equality is seldom achieved, yet providing an equitable opportunity base through education is achievable.

Chapter 4

The Complexity of Race and Socioeconomic Status

Remember, remember always, that all of us, and you and I especially, are descended from immigrants and revolutionists.

—Franklin D. Roosevelt, remarks before the Daughters of the American Revolution, Washington, DC, April 21, 1938, from *The Public Papers and Addresses of Franklin D. Roosevelt, 1938*

Worcester has always been an immigrant town. Given the geographical location one might say it is a perfect example of the trends in immigration throughout the development of an American city. From settlement to post industrialization Worcester's racial demographics reflect the shifts in demographics seen across the United States of America. Examining the student population from 1885–1915 we see that in 1885, 5,020 of the town's school children were born to American parents while 5,841 were born to immigrants. In 1895 the numbers increase to 7,183 and 8,072 respectively. In 1915 the numbers increase once again to 9,486 and 14,299. During the period of 1885–1920, students born to foreign parents were predominantly from the countries of Ireland, Sweden, Canada, and Russia. There is also a documented surge of students from Italian born parents after 1910. Thus, in the early to mid-1900s, only one hundred years ago, the majority of Worcester's population was either immigrants or first generation Americans (Sullivan 1920).

According to a study conducted by the Central Massachusetts Regional Planning District (1967), the population of Worcester continued to climb steadily throughout the early 1900s. In 1920 Worcester's population stood at 179,754; in 1930 it rose to 195,311; in 1940 the population dropped slightly to 193,694; and in 1950 the population rose again to 203,486. Thus, by 1950 the industrialized factory city of Worcester was clearly a growing city dominantly comprised of white European immigrants. By 1950, the city of

Worcester was in reality 99.2 percent white (Worcester Regional Research Bureau Inc. 2001). There was also a small population of African Americans in Worcester in 1950 which, as Thomas Del Prete (2010) suggests have been in the area since antebellum days. These statistics are important, for there is a paucity of student ethnic data reports by the city from the 1930s to the 1960s. This deficiency highlights Worcester's perception of itself as an all-white city. However, it is also important to note that, within what appeared to be a solid white population, especially as the civil rights movements of the 1950s and 1960s began to form, the neighborhoods of Worcester clearly reflected the Irish, Swedish, French-Canadian, and Italian roots of its citizens and these citizens maintained a strong sense of ethnic identity and pride.

By 1960 we see the continuing effect of the robust white ethnic immigrant surge from Europe during the 1870–1920 time periods. The population of Worcester slightly declined during the 1950s and stood at 186,587 in 1960. Of this population, 184,280 were identified as white, resulting in a city population that was 98.76 percent white dropping only slightly from 99.2 percent ten years earlier; the school system reflected this on the micro level. Thus, on April 2, 1964, the same year Burncoat Senior High came into operation the *Evening Gazette* reported that the student population in Worcester consisted of 30,125 white and 643 nonwhite pupils. Therefore, in 1964 the student population of Worcester was 98 percent white (Survey Shows 643 Nonwhites in Schools 1964). This stands in stark contrast to 2010–2011; with a student population of 24,192 the Worcester public schools had a 63.5 percent minority and 36.5 percent white student population, a dramatic shift in a forty-five-year span.

Again, if we analyze Worcester's population even further, in 1960 the population was 13.2 percent foreign born and 45.2 percent first generation Americans. Indeed, although considered white, 58.4 percent of Worcester's population were either immigrants or first generation American primarily originating from the countries of Canada, Ireland, Italy, and Sweden. These numbers actually represent a sharp drop in comparison to the early 1900s. What is unmistakable is by the time Burncoat Senior High enters the Worcester School District, the majority of students are white with only a little over 2 percent of the total student population being ethnic minorities. The melting pot or "Americanization" philosophy and segregation that permeated the nation and the nation's schools was manifesting itself in Worcester, Massachusetts.

As documented, Worcester, now a city but once a town, was settled and founded by immigrants. A 2011 Worcester *Telegram and Gazette* article entitled "Changing Faces" documents the dramatic ethnic change of the Worcester population from 2000–2010, specifically the school population. However, the author fails to recognize that Worcester was always an ethnically diverse city; the demographic shift of late merely reflects a different immigrant population. The 1950s statistics that Worcester's population was 99 percent white is simply misleading; in fact the term "white" is problematic in and of itself.

White is a racial construction, just as is black and Latino. These categories serve to group individuals. One could argue that, historically, the primary purpose of these groupings was to segregate, penalize, or oppress certain populations. With the advent of the civil rights movements, the groupings were then used for affirmative action purposes. However, what remains clear is that identifying individuals based on these broad, socially created racial constructions often diminishes the ability for individuals to claim their ethnic identities or individual identities. These racial terms and categories imply that to be white or black or Latino means to share the same identity or, more specifically, the same culture, traditions, oppressions, or social benefits that being a member of that group affords. There are no continents or countries identified as Whiteland or the Republic of Black, nor do all Latinos originate from Latin America. Within these racial categories are individuals with ethnic and cultural identities. These ethnic and cultural identities do not only belong to those with melanin and pigmented skin; nor does being white inherently suggest an individual is devoid of ethnicity. The early Worcester school department of the 1800s understood this fact, as substantiated by their documentation of white ethnic immigrants in the public schools. However, given the sociohistoric context one can assume this acknowledgment and data collection was not done in an effort to embrace all ethnicities rather the data may have been used once again to separate, label, or force assimilation upon students.

PAINFUL SHIFTS

During the formative years of the Worcester Public School system, there was a clear push for the Americanization of students. The melting pot theory thrived in which white European immigrants were expected and encouraged to shed the culture from which they came and to melt into the fabric of the United States. Schools were instrumental in this process, as they were the socializing agent for immigrant children. With the very beginnings of elementary schools, bilingual teachers were placed into schools with large proportions of non-English speaking children in order to hasten the pace at which these students acquired the English language. Evening schools were established for adults and children alike with the end goal of socializing white ethnic immigrants to the mores of the United States. Worcester appeared to be successful in this endeavor. What the citizens of Worcester or the school department did not anticipate was the substantial ethnic transformation that would impact the city and the nation.

The racial and ethnic shifts taking place in Worcester had a substantial impact on the public school system. Within a decade after Burncoat Junior-Senior High opened its doors racial incidents were reported by the local newspaper, the *Telegram and Gazette*. The newspaper reported that although there were less than fifty Latino and black students amongst the nearly 1,200 students at Burncoat, race was a factor in many disputes (Police patrol starts at Burncoat schools 1974). In 1982, the district, well aware of the ethnic and cultural clash Burncoat was experiencing was successful in receiving a $20,000 Ford Foundation grant for school improvement. According to Principal John O'Malley, the money was to be used in increasing school and community awareness of the diverse ethnic makeup of the city (Burncoat to Get a $20,000 Foundation Grant 1982). Despite this grant and the good intentions of the principal and district, in 1983, the *Telegram* reported a fight between black and white students that resulted in three injured, including a student who was stabbed in the face with an umbrella. In 1986 Burncoat received funds to house a nursery on site for students with children and became the first high school in Worcester to have a facility for teenage mothers (Blezard 1986). Many correlated the teenage parent program to the increase in ethnic minorities and lower socioeconomic status students coming from Great Brook Valley thus reinforcing the negative stereotypes attributed to these students.

The racial unrest and tensions at Burncoat persisted into the 1990s. The district and school administration continued to work to improve school climate instituting a mediation program in 1989. During the first decade of the program 13,803 disputes were mediated and in 1999 the program received a $20,000 grant to continue the work of improving relations within the school (McNiff 1999). During the early twenty-first century there was an increased push toward small learning communities and small schools across the nation. Worcester received funding and Burncoat was to be part of this movement. The small schools movement's basic tenant was that small schools allowed for a stronger sense of community and stronger interpersonal relationships within the school which would positively impact student academic outcomes. However, seventy out of seventy-four staff members at Burncoat voted against the move to small schools within the school arguing that much of what the small schools movement purports to accomplish was already being done at Burncoat through various programs (McFarlane 2005). That same year Burncoat would also garner another historic distinction, however, this one even more dubious than those in the past.

In October of 2005 a riot involving over sixty students would take place at Burncoat Senior High. Leaving five injured, including four staff. Fifteen students would be legally charged, nineteen would be suspended, and twelve would not return to the school. This would be the first time in Worcester Public School history that one incident would result in the expulsion of more than ten students (Reis 2005). This riot would also have racial undertones, with staff referring to it as "the race riot"; and it would serve to further complicate relationships within the school and community.

The impact of race on the students at Burncoat Senior High is yet to be fully realized. What is evident is that students at Burncoat Senior High feel they are learning in a discriminatory environment at best. While many students stated they appreciate Burncoat Senior High for the diversity of the student population they acknowledge that the day to day operation at Burncoat is based on a separate and not equal practice.

Why discrimination and segregation is happening at such a diverse urban school is debatable according to the students. Some blame the teachers:

I don't like talking about race, like students' races, it seems wrong and old. But so many teachers here are racist. How can you have no patience for children and be a racist and still be a teacher?

It's the school they keep the drama going, as a white person I never get stopped in the halls for a pass.

One teacher always says if you want to speak Spanish go back to where you came from.

I get stopped for a pass and they don't. I get comments on my clothes, they don't. It's because I'm black.

An incident that occurred while some of the students were at Burncoat Senior High fed into the belief that the school seeks to segregate and oppress the minority student population. A white staff member at the school called a black male student a ni**er. The staff member was allowed to remain in his position with little consequence. This is fact; however, the incident has taken on a life of its own over the years with the story being elaborated on through Facebook pages and hallway conversations. The reality, despite the elaboration, is that an adult authority figure called an adolescent male a vulgar, derogatory, demeaning name historically associated with slavery and oppression. This reality calls into question what message this sends to the Burncoat Senior High community, indeed, what did and should Burncoat students have taken away from this incident?

LEARNING

Much of our learning takes place in schools during our most formative years. This learning is not isolated to academics; rather it includes our thoughts and beliefs regarding racial equity and justice. "The transmission of culture is the primary task of the educational system of a society" (A. Ornstein 2003, 167). With President Bush in 2002 clearly outlining seven secular character education traits into legislation including civic virtue, respect, and caring, the school's role in character education became even more solidified (Spring 2005). Theorists and educators from the days of Thomas Jefferson and John Dewey to present day Theodore Sizer and Jeannie Oakes all agree that for all students (of the day) to reach their full potential as individuals and citizens and for society to flourish the public school system must play a large role in the socialization process (Dewey 1916; Jefferson 1893; Sizer 1985; Oakes and Lipton 2007). The United States compulsory public education system has gone through many transformations. Ultimately, in its present incarnation the compulsory school system is intended to generate a skilled labor force equipped to compete on a global level; and to create a culturally and socially literate population able to think critical and contribute to society (U.S. Department of Education n.d.). This deviates only slightly from almost one hundred years ago when the NEA stated "education in democracy, both within and without the school, should develop in each individual the knowledge, interests, ideals, habits, and powers whereby he will find his place and use that place, to shape both himself and society toward ever nobler ends" (Commission on the Reorganization of Secondary Education 1918, 18).

We learn through observation, reinforcement and punishment as children (i.e., Bandura and Pavlov's theories on Social Cognitive Learning and Conditioning). Children mimic adult behavior both in language and action. Children learn what is and is not appropriate from concrete punishment, a particular glance from an adult, accolades, or a simple smile. If they observe others behaving poorly without consequence or at times rewarded they too may imitate the behavior. Teachers and school staff are given the immense challenge of educating our youth. As adults interacting with children on a daily basis they are not only educators, they are role models, and they are ultimately socializing agents (Bryant and Zimmerman 2003). Socializing children is not their sole responsibility, however, their role as educators makes it imperative that school staff recognize the pivotal role they play and remain conscious of this fact regardless of number of years in the profession or the demands placed on them by the educational system or society as a whole. Without proper socialization, given chasms in beliefs and behavior, anarchy will ensue and society will fail to function as a whole.

VERBAL POLLUTION

The example above typifies the continuation of cultural incompetency in our schools and in this case a specific crisis of verbal pollution. Verbal pollution in this context refers to the usage of words and comments that the majority agrees are offensive and at times damaging that may lead to the deterioration of certain social institutions. By all accounts this student and staff member had a relatively good relationship. So what occurred in this moment? Speculation is just that, teachers instantly took to the defense of the staff member claiming he was attempting to be hip and relate to the student using his own vernacular. Others speculated that this educator was ignorant and a racist. I argue that this educator unknowingly was a participant in verbal pollution.

Much like being in a park or lake littered with trash we are more likely to drop a gum wrapper or not force our children to pick up the napkin they dropped. This is not necessarily a conscious act to pollute. However, the result is the same regardless of intent, the park or lake becomes polluted. The school is a microcosm of society, thus bearing the same societal ills. The pollution we see in schools is often literal and similar to the park or parking lot. Even more damaging to the school are the other forms of pollution that are growing at an alarming rate such as intolerance, swearing, derogatory slurs, and basic lack of respect for one another as human beings. Much like the polluted park or lake, the schoolhouse has become a receptacle for more pollution. Students, teachers, and administrators see and hear the pollution on a daily basis and they eventually begin to add to the pollution, some consciously, most unconsciously. The polluted park and lake are no places for our children to play at or swim in for health and safety reasons. The same can be said about the polluted school. The polluted school is incongruent to learning and teaching. It creates a hostile environment for all present.

All members of the school community must work together to clean up the pollution. The cleanup will not be effective if it is done in isolation by one segment of the community. If done together and with understanding, all within the school will take away a deeper knowledge of the societal ills that plague the school and have a deeper respect for one another. This respect in combination with the pride gained from having a "clean" school will ultimately create a better learning environment, improving academic achievement and interpersonal relationships amongst the ever increasingly diverse ethnic school body.

As one student noted, "Many of the kids here are racist and cruel and many of the teachers don't do anything about it. They constantly swear and talk to the teachers and use the 'N' word all the time." If this remains the culture of the school, if pollution continues to grow, the task of educating students at Burncoat will become impossible. This school, like many others in the United States, was ill prepared to deal with the flash demographic shift that has transpired over the past twenty years. The teaching force remains predominantly white and middle class while the urban student population steadily increases in diversity. The common use of racist and sexist language in the hallways of Burncoat Senior High and this staff member's use of the N-word is only the beginning of the consequences manifested by this cultural clash and incompetence.

Another consequence of the perceived segregation and discrimination at Burncoat Senior High is the internalization of negative stereotypes by the students. Indeed, students have strong feelings about race and how it impacts the school community. The students, however, do not only blame the staff, they take some responsibility for the segregation. As one stated, "They closed Caf C to force integration because we self-separate. But go to the D wing, it's little Puerto Rico." This student is referring to the fact that the school administration acknowledged years prior that the cafeterias were self-segregated by various student ethnic groups. In order to force integration cafeteria c was closed, this did little to integrate the student body. Equally troubling is the turning of student ethnic groups against one another.

> As Julia stated "The Puerto Ricans act like they're better than blacks!" Steven added "Latinos think fighting is the way to deal with differences." Julia, an articulate ethnic minority female headed to an Ivy League university noted "I was bullied severely as a freshman. Now as a senior you learn to cooperate and get along. I don't know . . . is disrespect a race issue? I don't know. I see a large segment of white students being disrespectful. Then I see the worst examples of stereotypes among the blacks and Latinos. In the end I wonder how some people are raised." Jonathan and Jose lingered after everyone left and Jonathan added "My problem is more with students who are racist about Puerto Ricans. I just wanted all these kids to be honest when they say it's loud in the college prep classes, and fight and stuff, just be honest and say its Puerto Ricans. You know because it is. You don't know, I see white people all the time and I want to do what they're doing, but I just can't."

Jonathan was angry about the racism he sees directed toward his ethnic group but struggled because he also believes much of what the other students were saying was accurate. He spoke of wanting to be like the white students in a dreamy sort of way and his status as a Puerto Rican as an innate limitation that he cannot overcome. He had resolved to make the best of his education at Burncoat Senior High and his destiny as a Puerto Rican male. As one student noted "The way we're treated, the way we separate, what classes the blacks and Puerto Ricans are in, it's all a self-fulfilling prophecy."

Many of these students have fallen victim to the self-fulfilling prophecy and adopted a philosophy of doing their time at Burncoat Senior High, accepting their dismal academic performance and educational experience as destiny rather than choice. The apathy is not surprising as only 33 percent of students at Burncoat feel all of their teachers want them to do their best. Overwhelmingly, the students who believe this are white.

Although students recognize discriminatory treatment, on average 65 percent of Burncoat students feel like they are treated fairly. This is a high number considering the racial disparities that have been outlined. However, given the internalization of negative stereotypes, these students often feel they are treated as they deserve to be treated, regardless of if the treatment is poor. It is not only the minority students at Burncoat who recognize inequity; white students readily acknowledge a difference in treatment as well.

> Jody stated "I see a difference, as a white person I notice I don't get stopped in the hall for a pass. Another thing I see is that like in classes, Julia is typically the only black girl in all our AP classes. I know there are other smart black people!"

As a consequence of the strife between ethnic groups in combination with normal adolescent behaviors bullying is normative at Burncoat Senior High. Coming into ninth grade 30 percent of students reported having been bullied and 27 percent reported that they have bullied another student. However, for those who were entering tenth, eleventh, and twelfth grade the numbers rose dramatically to 52 percent of the population reporting having been a victim of bullying and 49 percent having engaged in bullying behavior toward fellow students.

These students—white, black, Latino—have internalized many of the stereotypes that are being displayed and reinforced in the walls of Burncoat Senior High. The confluence of these stereotypes, self-segregation, and the segregation along academic tracks and the magnet program only serve to increase the collateral damage on the students, staff, and community. The damage is already evident through self-reports by students. Given the diversity of the school, it is shocking that 28 percent of students at Burncoat Senior High report that they never work with or talk to someone of a different race or cultural background at school. The separation of students along ethnic and cultural lines only serves to once again reinforce fear and stereotypes amongst students.

ACADEMIC IDENTITY: CHOICE OR LABEL?

The complexity of race matters at Burncoat Senior High is not an isolated phenomenon. As a student noted, we may prefer not to talk about race, to believe it is a historical problem, and we are, after the election of President Obama, a post-racial America, but this would be a false belief. Indeed, it would be a damaging belief, for it would limit our exploration of solutions. Much research has been conducted regarding ethnic minority student achievement.

Possibly the most widely referenced authors on Black student achievement is John Ogbu. Ogbu and Fordham's (1986) article on the burden of acting white focuses on the pressures black students may feel in regard to choosing between academic failure and success. Based on the historical status of African American people in the United States, African American students may experience a disconnect and limit investment in academics. Ogbu acknowledges that one cannot generalize to an entire population, and there is variation in terms of coping mechanisms within the African American population. The experience of African Americans in the United States differs from other ethnic groups for several reasons. The involuntary entrance into the United States through the system of slavery produced a system of racial stratification. Racial stratification in this society has led to increased levels of poverty, unemployment, and substandard education within the African American community. Ogbu, much like Roscigno (1998), offers the suggestion that Black people are at a disadvantage in this society and do not have the same economic opportunities as white Americans. As a result, some black individuals may not see the value of education as a means to obtaining financial stability or social mobility.

According to Ogbu, African American students view education as a tool useful for white people in U.S. society, leading black students to attribute doing well in school to white students only. In order to keep their own identity and not be accused of acting "white," they choose to not perform as well as they could in school (Ogbu and Fordham 1986). The authors suggest that African American students are concerned with being accused of acting "white" and this concern impacts academic achievement. Black students may limit themselves academically in order to fit in with their peers. Yet, many black and Latino students at Burncoat view education as a means to success for all students, it is accessibility to appropriate and useful education that serve to be the barriers for these students. They cite the structure of the classroom and teaching style as impediments to their learning. The over-populated classrooms are a distraction for both high and underachieving students at Burncoat. State mandated tests and the associated pressure of teachers to cover all necessary test-related material has resulted in confusion and less time for student questions in class. These responses correlate with a study conducted several years earlier in another local high school (Fisher 2005).

Ogbu (1991) suggests minority groups adapt differently to U.S. society based on how a particular minority group entered into the United States. He presents the idea of voluntary minorities, who come to this country voluntarily seeking to fulfill the "American Dream," and involuntary minorities who were forced to become members of American society through slavery or colonization. Ogbu believes that involuntary minorities such as African Americans suffer from low effort syndrome.

Ogbu suggests that African American students do not have the academic success of other minority groups or white students due in part to their socio-historical experience in the United States. During slavery, individuals of African descent were involuntary minorities brought to the United States and who were placed into a subordinate "caste" position system in society. A job ceiling was put in place that denied African American individuals access to upward social mobility. Therefore, many African American individuals developed a belief system and coping mechanisms that discounted formal education as a tool for social mobility. For decades many non-immigrant (involuntary) African American adults have been denied jobs and placed into subordinate positions in U.S. society; thus, they developed coping mechanisms in order to make sense of the situation.

Ogbu also suggests that an oppositional identity and culture has developed based on the history of most Blacks in the United States. Ogbu clarifies the concept of oppositional identity by utilizing using the term cultural inversion. Cultural inversion refers to the process whereby symbols, whether it be dress or language, and behaviors that are associated with a dominant culture are deemed inappropriate for a subordinate culture. Cultural inversion eventually leads to an "alternative cultural frame of reference," meaning some African American individuals have a different set of values than Whites (J. Ogbu 1991, 441). Many African American students may attribute academics, doing well in school, and the use of standard English as "acting white." Historically, African American individuals have been unable to succeed as a whole in white culture. In order to cope, African American students have their own ideal in which they emulate and promote. Students that do succeed in school are often forced to have a double consciousness or hide their success in order to avoid being accused of "acting white." Burncoat students do not exemplify this philosophy. Indeed, these students are not fearful of acting white; rather they expressed annoyance with both the staff and some of their fellow students for what they perceive to be unequal treatment of all students.

Ogbu claims the Black experience in the United States has contributed to the failure of many African American students. Based on the historical experiences of African American parents in our society, parents often pass on to their children their own beliefs that society will not reward black students' educational accomplishments as much as they do white students' accomplishments. If this is transpiring in some Burncoat students' homes, the unequal treatment that takes place at Burncoat only serves to magnify and justify the expectations of bias.

While I agree with Ogbu's assessment of voluntary and involuntary immigrant populations, I would argue most of the black and Latino students at Burncoat did not focus on white individuals, nor did they gauge their academic successes or failures on "whiteness." These students did not make a conscious choice of academic failure or academic success. Rather, these students want to be successful in areas that they believe are accessible. This is not due to the development of an oppositional identity, a lack of motivation, or low effort; rather it is the result of concrete life experiences that have denied them access to social capital as well as, in the case of Burncoat, educational access to rigorous academic material, and engaged faculty. These students are ambitious and may only exhibit Ogbu's "low effort syndrome" as it relates to academics because the educational system has divested, and ultimately failed to fulfill its obligation to these students.

In fact, since the late nineteen-nineties studies have repeatedly shown that many ethnic minorities, in particular black students, are actually more optimistic about future employment than white students, and they also perceive education as key to getting these jobs at a higher percent than white students. Indeed, these ethnic minority students have more positive attitudes toward school than their white classmates and often have a higher level of engagement than their white peers (Ainsworth-Darnell and Downey 1998; Shernoff and Schmidt 2008). This can be seen at Burncoat with the class of 2010, the black student population's graduation rate was 3 percent higher than the white student subgroup (Massachusetts Department of Elementary and Secondary Education 2010). This seemingly contradictory piece of data may be explained by particular ethnic minority students recognizing that they do not have the social capital to rely on therefore they must utilize education as a means to success. A daunting question that lingers is if these ethnic minority students are more engaged and more positive about school than their white peers, why then are they failing to succeed? While black students are beginning to make some academic gains the institutionalized racism that still permeates much of America's institutions, including the educational system continues to be impactful on the academic and social development of all students.

Of great concern within educational circles is the continuing deficit in educational outcomes and achievement amongst the Latino student population. In the United States, one in four k–12 public school children are Latino (The Commission for Latino Educational Excellence 2011). Latino students are growing in numbers in our secondary education system however they persistently have a high drop-out rate and some of the lowest test scores. Nationally, only about half of Latino high school students graduate in four years (Swail, Cabrera and Lee 2004). Burncoat's class of 2010 reflected national norms with only 53 percent of Latino students and 48 percent of English language learners graduating with their class (Massachusetts Department of Elementary and Secondary Education 2010). Studies have been conducted that show that Latinos are often mislabeled and have improper placement in academic tracks due to assumptive behavior by school staff. These assumptions also place Latinos at a disadvantage as school staff often adopts the philosophy that Latinos are not real Americans deserving of their best efforts. Rather they are seen as population of immigrants making their jobs as teachers more difficult. Their apathetic treatment is then internalized by the Latino students (Cammarota 2006). Given the exponential growth of these subgroups in the United States this gap must be addressed. While America took hundreds of years to provide some semblance of equity to black individuals, America does not have the same luxury of time in this case. Failure to provide equitable educational resources to the Latino and English language learners in our society without a doubt will have an irreversible impact on the trajectory of American society.

While the history of exclusionary and race based segregation in the United States is well documented there is another form of segregation that has a tremendous impact on American students. That is segregation between schools as well as within schools based on socioeconomic status. Socioeconomic status (SES) refers to an individual's or family's status in relation to attainment in three domains: education, income, and occupation. Exploration of socioeconomic status is important as these three attributes in combination often dictate the level of power, on multiple dimensions, that individuals possess. Principal Foley recognizes the complexity of socioeconomic status as it relates to all who live within the walls of Burncoat Senior High:

> The lives of these kids are so complex. I had four years as an assistant principal (at another local school) and now four years at Burncoat as principal. I have a better understanding of the lives of these kids outside of school and the impact on their ability to "do school." Probably more aptly put their inability to "do school." These kids have tough lives; I don't know how some of them make it out of bed in the morning. It's not about race it's about economics. I see a much greater social mixing of ethnicities then I did when I was a student here. But the other factor is still there. (Principal Foley)

SOCIOECONOMIC STATUS

As noted in chapter 3 over 59 percent of Burncoat Senior High students are classified as low-income, or low socioeconomic status. There are educational consequences for students that come from low socioeconomic communities as research has shown a correlation between academic achievement and socioeconomic status (Orr 2003). Children from lower socioeconomic families often have fewer academic resources within the home, such as books or computers. In addition, families of lower socioeconomic status often do not have the financial resources to aid students in academic distress, such as hiring tutors or placing children in enrichment activities. These foundational issues result in students from lower SES homes on average having a slower rate of language acquisition skills as well as mathematical competency. Lower SES students are nearly 50 percent more likely to have learning related problems in comparison to their higher SES counterparts. Given this, students from low SES families enter high school over three grade levels behind their higher SES peers. Unfortunately, this trend continues in high school with lower SES students graduating from high school four grade levels behind their higher SES peers (Palardy 1998). Low SES students in turn have lower college graduation rates and less earning power. This not only impacts these students, but the entire economy of the United States.

As if the very real disparity between students of differing SES was not enough to impact their academic experiences, studies have also shown that teachers view students from higher SES families in a more favorable light in comparison to students from lower SES families. Teachers who adopt this stance often view the students' SES as a variable that is not only out of their control, but a variable that precludes students from academic success. This philosophy in turn limits the effort put forth in educating this population, resulting in the reinforcement of low achievement. Complicating matters even further, is the fact that children attending school in lower SES communities often have the most inexperienced teachers to educate this complex population (Auwarter and Aruguete 2008).

Educational setbacks, limited resources, and lack of teacher support have a direct impact on students' educational aspirations and achievement. Just as it relates to race, as low SES students become disillusioned with the educational system and see no chance of upward mobility, they often disengage with academics resulting in academic underachievement. However, what is imperative to understand when examining the consequences of low SES and poverty on student achievement is that is it not predestined, nor does it have to be an insurmountable barrier for these students. While there are some hurdles to overcome research has also shown that parental and family expectations regarding education can overcome the impact of low SES (Berzin 2010). Therefore, while teachers have a role in removing stereotypes and bias as it pertains to their teaching and expectations, parents, families, and the entire community have a responsibility to set a high level of expectation for their children and cannot simply leave the responsibility of educating children in the hands of educators.

The expectations and stereotypes related to socioeconomic status have impacted the students at Burncoat. Just as there appears to be separation and segregation along ethnic lines there also appears to be one along SES. This is not surprising given the discussion of neighborhood and the two distinct neighborhoods from which students enter Burncoat. In addition, some of the students within the magnet opt into Burncoat from other SES neighborhoods.

Therefore, what we see are students from higher SES backgrounds being placed in the higher ability tracks. One may argue this is a consequence of the academic deficits lower SES students possess upon entering high school. Others may argue it is a consequence of teacher bias, low expectations of low SES students, and favoritism toward higher SES students. Regardless of where one places the responsibility what remains clear is that it is reinforcing separation amongst the student population. In fact, 32 percent of Burncoat Senior High students report that they never work with, or talk to, someone of a different socioeconomic status. This number suggests a higher level of segregation along socioeconomic lines than racial segregation at Burncoat. This segregation can serve to reinforce stereotypes and limit access to peer role models. In addition low SES students may internalize their placement in a lower track as an innate ability limitation associated with low SES. This attribution would then result in apathy amongst students directly impacting academic achievement. Ultimately, this isolation is having an impact on the educational experience of all students as well as the staff at Burncoat Senior High. Burncoat is reflective of what is transpiring in the district and national level.

I have to stand back and recognize that class is as great an impediment as race. So I think the big issue for public education is how do we take the reins for what we signed on as educators to do? So when I talk about the current Worcester Public School context, it's this: when only about 30 percent of our students are meeting the benchmarks in aggregate that is a whole district story. That's not just a story for Main South or the Burncoat quadrant. It's a story for the Doherty quadrant, the west side, for everybody. You're right about the small school's movement; Gates acknowledges that changing structure without changing relationships will not get the results. If you study deeply reform and restructure, roles and relationships is very key and very clearly defined as making a difference in success at the high school level. And so there is all that has gone on, we talk about what's happening outside of the teaching and learning realm. We have standards and accountability on the state and federal level. And then I've heard from all of the principals that there are some of the needs our children and families have given the demographics. One of the greatest strengths in relation to the act (NCLB) is the conversation around wrap around services. That's the reason I had for two consecutive years with these partnership meetings how can we leverage your wonderful resources with our needs in a meaningful way? Not just in terms of having a lot of people showing up. We've had the thousand points of light with no impact. That's what I'm excited about working with partners for wrap around services. The academic needs are so great that we need to focus on what we're best at. We need other to support the other needs. Those are the conversations we have to have to help principals and help students. We are glad four schools received wrap around funding through race to the top. For it (community partnerships) to really add value and have meaning we need to sit down as partners. The greatest partnerships are those that are built together. I have to build some conversations. The settlers, the immigrants of 2011 are not different from the immigrants of 1911 except they look different so how do we use that to bridge the gap. Every corner in Worcester has a church that represents the ethnicity of different cultures. We have to build bridges, it's what I say to folks now the Puerto Ricans, Dominicans, Africans Iranians, African Americans have as much pride as past immigrants. We can get training for our staff but once we have cultural competence how do we expect anything different? We're just willing a difference. If we bring in Dr. Fisher how does it change after she leaves? Training is a technical response, courageous conversations around race and class, some of this work can reinforce stereotypes. The community has to be ready and willing to acknowledge . . . one of the fears of mine coming to Worcester was that I was going to raise race as an issue. Everyone expected me to play the race card. With 70 percent of my children failing I don't have to play the race card. This is an all child conversation. But in a lot of ways it's still race issue. My Latino population is the largest enrolled group in the Worcester Public Schools. But when I look within the achievement levels whites, who are free or reduced lunch are not achieving any better than my children of color who are receiving free and reduced lunch so it really does become a class issue. (Superintendent Boone)

The tensions of who knows best and makes policy also are a national issue that is playing out in the Worcester public schools. Quite often the voices of minority parents and lower socioeconomic communities are disconnected. While the middle and upper class white voices are heralded as all knowing. Case in point in Worcester, parents at a local, largely minority and low income, elementary school voted to adopt uniforms. Several school committee members publically opposed the parents' plan. This was a pivotal moment at this underperforming school as Superintendent Boone noted:

The uniforms in themselves do not impact student achievement. In their home country they wore uniforms they saw it as a respect and a sense of pride. So when you really talk about parent engagement, this is a moment where parents are saying we want to be fully engaged. I spend time with these parents, the uniforms became a point for Latino parents African parents and others finding commonalities. It is a no harm no foul decision. It builds community and culture. This sense of community allows kids to be successful. Look at University Park Campus School, a sense of community. I learned during my transition visits, and met with the faculty at UPCS, a group of students. These kids were very clear, the teachers made the strong point to us that we will not fail that we can be successful, and we can't give up on ourselves because they will not give up on us. Tell me about your grades. Some did as good, some did a bit better, one African-American boy had this look on his face, he said "hmm before I came here I didn't do anything in school and nobody made me. I told teachers I didn't want to do anything and the teachers said fine don't. But I came here and the very first time I didn't turn in the assignment the teacher said yes you will." And every day after school the teacher helped him understand that he could do it and helped him understand. Building a sense of community makes a difference in the school. If you look at UPCS we know their beating all odds. High rates of ELL, poverty, but they still build a sense of community for those kids. You can find it in a huge high school too, take a Worcester Tech, there's a sense of culture, pride, and community in that school. That's the real story, how do we create that. You have to be respectful of the diversity that comes in there. I know I ticked off people when I say of course I want diversity in my teaching ranks, but first I want teachers who care.

The concept of American individualism and meritocracy discussed as it pertains to neighborhood also has an impact on the gaps we see in academic achievement along racial and socioeconomic lines. These concepts ascribe failures and successes to individual motivation and choices. American individualism and meritocracy remove institutionalized racism and classism from the discussion of academic underachievement. This is an extremely dangerous practice as it serves to reinforce detrimental stereotypes amongst educators and students, with only negative consequences as a product. When educators remove responsibility of educating certain populations of students based on predetermined standards they not only place these students in peril but they gravely endanger the functioning of our society as a whole and America's place in the world economy.

CONCLUSION

The United States of America is becoming increasingly diverse. While the United States still remains 72.4 percent white, the black population is 12.6 percent, an increase of 12.3 percent since 2000; the Asian population is 4.8 percent, an increase of 43.3 percent since 2000; and the Hispanic population is 16.3 percent, an increase of 43 percent since 2000. Also, those who reported being bi- or multiracial increased by 32 percent since 2000. In fact, the growth in the Hispanic population accounts for nearly 50 percent of the American population growth from 2000–2010. The United States also is facing great economic challenges. In 2010, 15 percent of Americans were living in poverty; this translates to 46 million Americans. Twenty-two percent of all children under the age of eighteen in the United States are living in poverty (U.S. Census Bureau 2010). The devastating consequences of undereducating ethnic minorities and lower socioeconomic communities are such that the United States of America cannot afford to take the risk.

Superintendent Boone, and her administrative team as well as the Worcester School Committee are faced with the difficult task of utilizing budgetary resources to mitigate the effect of race and poverty on students and schools. Unfortunately, these two bodies often have divergent thinking when deciding on how best to proceed. As noted Dr. Boone has faced great criticism for her attention to level four schools, and the 70 percent of students that are not proficient according to MCAS and NCLB. The criticism often comes from the 30 percent, the white or middle to upper middle class families. This population has accused the administration of neglecting the needs of successful students and schools. Dr. Boone is quick to note that she has preserved class sizes and has not taken away from successful schools and students. Rather, by dedicating resources toward underperforming schools the administration is supporting the healthy growth and development of the entire school district. Dr. Boone recognizes the need for more advanced placement opportunities and programs for the gifted but she will not support these programs as another tool that will be used to separate and segregate students based on class and ethnicity. The perception that all resources are being moved away from these successful schools and communities has caused rumblings but not great middle class or white flight from the public schools, yet. As the reality sinks in that our nation's urban public schools are becoming increasingly minority and low income, with success and failure determined by testing, what will families who have the financial means choose to do with their children? And where will this leave the children and families who remain?

The issues related to poverty and the racial tensions seen across the United States are indicative of those faced in the Burncoat and Great Brook Valley neighborhood. These tensions and the associated consequences then permeate the high school. The issues manifesting themselves within the hallways of Burncoat Senior High are reflective of those seen in many urban communities. The question must be asked: Does the school, indeed the educational system have the tools to meet the challenges of America's changing face? Although the challenge is immense, the twenty-first century brought forward a renewed commitment by the school staff and district administrators to create a safe and academically sound community for the students at Burncoat. The staff and administration would refocus and take aim at building relationships, strengthening engagement, and attempting to reinforce the commitment of all to the improvement of the Burncoat Senior High community.

Chapter 5

Relationships Matter

A teacher who is attempting to teach without inspiring the pupil with a desire to learn is hammering on cold iron.

—Horace Mann, as quoted in *The Eclectic Magazine*
Vol. VII, (January–June 1868)

Communication, trust, and respect, are all necessary components of any healthy relationship. As human beings we all require and benefit from healthy interpersonal relationships not just with family members and friends but also with neighbors, employers, members of a church congregation, co-workers, and so on. Though all these relationships cannot be of the same intensity, every healthy relationship promotes and sustains our emotional, cognitive, and physical well-being. Failure to have such relationships can promote isolation, antisocial behavior, mental illness and ill health. Indeed, relationships matter.

Relationships are especially important to cultivate during adolescence, the period of development between childhood and adulthood when humans experience tremendous growth in biological, emotional, and cognitive development. While no definitive age boundaries mark the beginning and end of adolescence, the onset is typically regarded as beginning at puberty. The legal, rather than literal termination point is age eighteen. Most developmental theorists argue that the termination of adolescence is more fluid. It is, however, always marked by changes in reasoning, behavior, and the ability to care for oneself. During adolescence, individuals explore their multiple roles in multiple domains. Adolescents must accomplish this exploration while also attempting to manage dramatic hormonal shifts. While trying to comprehend these external and internal identity shifts, their brains continue to develop in ways that alter comprehension itself. Historians will quickly point out that prior to the twentieth century, "adolescence" wasn't even a term and the majority of humans in what we now call the teen years were not afforded the luxury of exploration. As laws governing the age of legal marriage suggest, these not yet fully mature humans were treated like adults by contemporary society's standards. That lack of distinction between the stages of human development had social and educational consequences, some negative, and some positive. But if the youth of yesterday were "forced to grow up," the adolescents of today are presented quite a conundrum; restricted by law and often by parental standards to still be children, they are faced with increasing societal pressure to contribute as adults. As Matthew noted "More kids have jobs now and they need the money, they have to work so there's no time to be involved at Burncoat." There's no time, in other words, to develop healthy relationships in their most sustained environment away from home: the school place.

Whereas the maturing person of earlier centuries was encouraged to sustain and expand healthy family relationships, many of today's public school students experience such unhealthy relationships at home that they become impediments to achievement at school. Perceptive adolescents know their peers suffer and in turn bring suffering to school with them. As Samuel noted, "A lot of these kids have problems at home, we need more therapists here." Given changing family demographics, a difficult economy and sky rocketing college costs, more and more adolescents confront ever-mounting financial and emotional responsibilities. Lacking strong relationships with adults to anchor them, adolescents undergo emotional, hormonal, and cognitive changes while struggling with often traumatic day to day life events. That combination of the biological, the psychological, and the social leads many adolescents to feel isolated and overwhelmed.

This sense of pressure and the subsequent stress faced by adolescents is magnified by the many high stake decisions that are presented to them at an increasingly young age. Well before ninth grade, students confront questions such as what do you want to do when you get older? How do you plan to make it happen? Such questions attribute a kind of autonomy or control to the adolescent which he or she cannot feel or have validated. Under such circumstance, the stress and confusion of the adolescent becomes palpable and often breaks through as disruptive behavior. The teachers and administrators at Burncoat Senior High School experience this complex dynamic in ways that mirrors their students' confusion. Expected to coexist as adults with adolescents for six hours a day, for 180 days a year, to transmit knowledge and cultivate skills so that these young strangers will pass state mandated tests and graduate in four years wears down even the most dedicated teacher. The pressure and stress that impact the students is also impacting the staff at Burncoat Senior High. The stress they experience taints the very ideals that led them to become teachers and often leads to an undiagnosed resentment of the general student body. Unhealthy relationships do not excuse underperformance by teachers or students, though such relationships—or, rather, the lack of healthy ones—may explain much of the problem. The complex rules that govern nature and current social expectations mandate that the teachers are the adults. Therfore in order to fulfill the educational mandate set forth by NCLB and the state of Massachusetts and also to regain a sense of job satisfaction, teachers and administrators must first figure out how to engage students. They must initiate a healthy relationship.

ENGAGEMENT

In order to succeed academically, students first must be engaged with the learning process. Engaged students have higher achievement levels and academic outcomes in comparison to their disengaged peers. Academic engagement is a "psychological investment in, and effort directed toward learning, understanding, or mastering the knowledge, skills, or crafts that academic work is intended to promote" (Newmann 1992, 12). According to Newman, academic engagement arises out of a need for competence in combination with an appreciation for school membership and recognition for authentic work.

School membership may be defined as the extent to which students see schooling as "legitimate." For the adolescent, legitimacy translates into a basic question: How fair are their teachers? Adults might better translate that concern into a series of more sophisticated questions such as, how clear is the purpose of schooling? Do the students get appropriate personal support? Is the system caring? The adolescent's perception of assigned work as "authentic" connects to extrinsic rewards. The adult should ask, does the process of schooling provide attainable rewards and means toward success? Most importantly, students need to develop an intrinsic interest or a connection to the material being studied so that they may then internalize the knowledge and construct new meaning. Students ask the question: Is there a connection between schooling and the real-world? Teachers should ask: Do I model how important teaching is to me and the world? The "world" should show students and teachers how highly it regards their mutual engagement with learning; the unhealthy relationship that has evolved between America and it's educators compounds the work of over-stressed teachers, but adjusting that attitude is the work of civic action. Thankfully, however, that work may begin by good teachers educating better citizens in the classroom, engaging students in a process teachers once affirmed as their own constitution.

How do we know student engagement when we see it? A construct of engagement based on behavior and affect has been proposed by Hudley et al.

(2003). According to Hudley, engagement can be viewed on two levels: behavioral and affective. Behavioral engagement refers to actions that the students adopt in order to remain a part of the schooling process. These actions include: attending regularly, avoiding conflict, respecting rules, and completing academic tasks. Affective engagement relates to the emotions connected to the learning process and achievement, similar to Newman's concept of membership. Again, theory can roll into a question: Are students seeing achievement as valuable, useful, and enjoyable, or as a rote process? Overall, student engagement under models similar to Hudley's must be seen as a combination of behavioral, cognitive, and emotional variables (Fredricks, Blumenfeld, and Paris 2004). Put simplistically, total engagement would require a student to behave in a manner that supports learning, to feel generally happy about and interested in their academic experience, and be able to self-regulate these emotions and thoughts regarding learning and the schooling process.

Other educational psychologists take engagement one step further and incorporate Csikszentmihalyi's theory of FLOW and optimizing experiences. The theory of FLOW posits that in order to optimize an experience an individual must be challenged yet also possess the self-perception that they have enough skill to meet said challenge (Csikszentmihalyi 1996). Thus, in regards to students there must be a significant level of academic challenge in order to discourage boredom, yet the student must also have the academic foundation, skill level, and self-concept as to not develop apathy, itself a derivative of frustration. While students at Burncoat do not utilize this theoretical language, they readily acknowledge boredom and apathetic behaviors. Kenneth, an honors level student noted, "I find myself to be bored in class more than I should, it's not fun." In fact, only 42 percent of Burncoat students feel their classes challenge them academically. That figure is remarkable since 90 percent of the students feel they have the academic skills to do well at Burncoat. There is a clear disconnect between their self-concept, that is, belief about their academic skills, and their academic performance. Academic engagement is a complex construct; however it is one that merits a deeper understanding as this is a variable that can be enhanced in order to promote academic achievement among adolescents.

OTHER VARIABLES

Given the changing demographics in the United States, much of the recent research focuses on minority student achievement and strives to establish a causal relationship between academic failure within this population and such factors as innate racial and ethnic disparities or socioeconomic disadvantage.

Other studies examine qualities "low effort syndrome" and "poor academic self-concept." The racial demographics at Burncoat, ironically, now make that once colonial school a paradigm for an urban school that reflects the country's newer immigration patterns.

Much of the research on this topic focuses on males within the Latino and black student population (Bryant and Zimmerman 2003; Noguera 2003; Roderick 2003). The male population is especially at risk of academic disengagement and failure. Male ethnic minority adolescents face images of rappers, athletes, and gangsters, most of whom attribute success to anything but academics. Female minority students are also at risk. As adolescent females and ethnic minorities they cannot escape the realities of their lives as double minorities in the United States (Gaganakis 2006; Rollock 2007). Just as the minority male must often contend with images of the minority athlete or music icon, so too female adolescents are faced with stereotypical images of ethnic women on television, in videos, and through music and magazines. Minority male and female commercial success stories usually do not exemplify models that are compatible with academic success. While students learn from and internalize many of these stereotypes, in many instances the people they have interpersonal relationships with, that is, teachers and family, are not discussing issues of race and gender in a meaningful way in order to dispel the stereotypes (Ward 2000).

ATTRIBUTION THEORY

Students' perceptions of failure or underachievement and the explanations they derive as the root cause of their achievements or failures have a direct correlation to their motivation and engagement (Weiner 1990). Weiner asserts that three dimensions make up causal attributions that students ascribe to failure and success. The first is the locus: whether or not the cause of failure is internal to the individual or external; second is the stability: whether the cause is constant or can change; and last is controllability: the ability or inability of the individual to control the cause. Students who believe they have failed due to a stable, uncontrollable cause typically lack motivation and engagement. In their 1996 study of high school students, Sian, Lightbody, Stocks, and Walsh found that secondary girls attributed academic success to working hard and teachers' liking them. Boys attributed their success to luck, cleverness, and talent. This finding might suggest that girls more so than boys face problems when interpersonal connections with teachers are not found in the classroom. The attribution becomes stable and uncontrollable, and failure becomes a permanent result of a teacher's dislike for the student. Once a student has this attribution, one can assume that engagement is dissolved.

If, for example, ethnic minorities or females attribute their failures to being disliked by teachers because of their ethnicity and gender, these are traits that cannot be controlled or changed and motivation and engagement will surely be impacted. If these same students attribute their failure to the fact that the teacher has internalized false or inappropriate beliefs and societal predications regarding success and failure, students may then be able to take control of the situation and begin strategies to master their learning. However, it is important to note that anytime a student attributes failure to a teacher's bias, it has the great possibility of stunting the student's engagement and investment in achieving.

Students, high school students especially, need to be made aware of the disparities that exist in our society and the many hurdles and obstacles that stand between them and a successful future so that they can overcome rather than internalize failure. It is clear that without support and open dialogue, lack of this knowledge may turn into frustration and disillusionment. Vulnerable young students can succumb to hopelessness and become academically disengaged, ultimately leading to academic underperformance.

Discussion with students regarding the realities of American culture and their experiences as students within this culture is paramount. Open dialogue often leads to an increased awareness and a better understanding of one's own identity; this in turn leads to better academic performance (Ward 2000). By giving voice to adolescents and empowering them through dialogue, change may indeed take place. Previous research has shown that students who are disengaged do not necessarily have lower academic self-concept, in fact they believe they possess the necessary academic skills. However, they do not utilize or maximize these academic skills because they do not see a future benefit (Fisher 2005). Giving adolescent students a broader perspective of the social institutions in which they operate can expose the various systems of oppression and begin to alleviate the sense of powerlessness that many students experience.

FIGHTING FOR SUCCESS

The many causes of student disengagement I have discussed were concretely evident at Burncoat, our paradigmatic school. So too was evidence of which variables were well within the control of faculty and administrators if recognized and understood.

During my time at Burncoat I was fortunate to spend a year meeting with a group of remarkably outspoken, funny and talented, tenth grade Latino and African heritage female students. They had done well in middle school but had experienced precipitous drops in achievement since arriving at Burncoat

Senior High. My goal during these after school meetings was to get to know these students and their thoughts on why they were not as academically successful as they were in middle school as well as to serve as a role model. To that end, I held bi-weekly meetings and conducted a quantitative self-concept assessment during the course of the study. Self-concept refers to one's beliefs about their own abilities. This is different from self-esteem which refers to one's emotional response to these self-concept markers. For example, a student may feel they are not the best at math but still feel good about themselves; in this case their mathematical self-concept is not negatively impacting their self-esteem. When examining the data from the Burncoat students' self-concept assessments, I determined that their lowest markers came under the categories of emotional self-concept, physical abilities, parent relations, and the general school marker, that is, the relationships with teachers and administrators. The highest self-concept markers were in academic content areas of math and English language arts. The scores imply that the students believed they were capable in terms of academic content knowledge and cognitive abilities but struggled with interpersonal relationships.

The data provided from the self-concept assessment coincides with the information gathered during focus groups. One of the most insurmountable factors impeding these students' academic success at Burncoat Senior High were the interpersonal relationships with the adults in their lives, both at home and in school. They expressed trepidation regarding relationships within the school with teachers, administrators, and guidance counselors. They also expressed some unease regarding parental relations. In many cases their overall emotional stability was lower compared to the other self-concept scores. This data led to one unifying conclusion: the teens were beginning to disengage. They felt isolated and misunderstood; they expressed frustration and felt they had no allies within the school.

At the time of my analysis, there was only one teacher of color at Burncoat. Students noticed. As Heather stated ". . . even the Spanish teacher is white." In fact, in this large urban district with a nearly two-third minority student population, the teaching force remains nearly 90 percent white. The students discussed at length the lack of support from adults at the school. They were disheartened by the lack of minority teaching and administrative staff at the school. The girls especially saw the lack of minority role models to connect with as problematic. However, the fact that the girls took the lack of minority staff as a message of some sort from the school system was in itself revealing. While the girls failed to succinctly articulate their concerns, what was made clear was that they felt the lack of minority teaching and administrative staff reflected an opinion by the school that only white people were good enough to be educators.

Rather than receiving care in the school setting, the girls reported that their personal and academic interests were often dismissed by those who were in authority. Without apparent allies there were no role models or any one individual they felt they could turn to for support or advice. During early conversations "allies" were discussed as people of color by the girls, but discussion in the focus groups quickly turned to allies as adults who cared about student success both emotionally and academically, regardless of ethnic background. Therefore, the students, while feeling some sense of discrimination and ethnic bias from the school system, recognize that allies and good teachers do not have to look like them, they just need to care. Here, then, is a variable that existing school staff could immediately address while seeking greater diversity. Faculty and administrators could re-engage. That re-engagement itself would be easier for adults to initiate were they to understand its proper cause and the imperative that they take adult control of the situation.

> Alexis expressed interest in fashion design and lamented that the school and teachers gave her no support. She attempted to enroll in an art elective for two years and was turned away by both teacher and guidance counselor. In the focus groups, we discussed the need for art classes as well as math classes in order to be in the fashion design industry. Motivated by this discussion, Alexis took the initiative to talk with the guidance counselor regarding taking a more advanced math course. Unfortunately, she was encouraged to take a lower level math course by the counselor who did not pursue why Alexis sought such a challenge. Alexis felt powerless to change her fate. With the lack of allies compounded by lack of encouragement by the adults in the school, engagement is stunted.

A culture clash also seemed to impede students' academic engagement. Normative behavior in the students' families and neighborhoods was not being replicated within the school setting. Even those students who reported feeling that they were treated with respect in their neighborhoods and homes felt diminished at school. When describing the interactions they had with teachers and administrators, students used words such as "degrading" and "disrespectful." The girls expressed dismay and confusion that these adults demanded respect but refused to give any in return. Adults, on the other hand, who had come to expect that students act "like students" and teachers must "behave like teachers," seemed unaware that their notions of these roles were outdated, infantilizing, misunderstood—and ultimately one major source of academic disengagement. This matter of teacher attitude most probably derives not only from pre-set notions of the teacher's role but would also seem to be both the result and partial cause of teacher disengagement. Here we have another variable teachers could adjust.

"In my neighborhood respect is earned. . . ." Missy expressed her frustration of receiving a punishment for being "verbally aggressive" toward a teacher after he refused to let her use the ladies room "they think we are going to do something . . . like it's a big plan . . . I had to go . . . it was you know . . . that time . . . so I finally just got in his face and left."

Missy was suspended for two days. The girls were raised to respect authority however they were used to getting respect in return from the adults within their families and community. Such negotiable power equity was contradictory to the reactions from staff at Burncoat. Shocked that she had been denied a need nobody would question at home, Missy reacted to disrespect with disrespect.

The young women I met with most assuredly did have positive experiences with some teachers. After reviewing their responses, it also became clear that they showed admiration and respect for two very different types of teachers. The first were those who were well-versed in their subject content areas; the other were those teachers that attempted to relate to the students on a personal level. A close analysis of student responses, moreover, made clear that the teachers who displayed expertise succeeded in winning student admiration when they made it clear they respected their students enough to care that they learned.

> Takia said about one such teacher ". . . he really knows what he is talking about and he tries to make me understand . . . man I don't get it sometimes . . . but he keeps trying." Another well-liked teacher mentioned by Mariah stood in stark contrast to the first ". . . that lady is crazy! I haven't learned nothing this year in that class . . . but it's cool she always asks about us and what's going on and we talk about real stuff. . . ."

The students readily admitted to putting in more academic effort for both of these kinds of teachers while acknowledging that putting in effort for teachers that already dislike you is a waste of time and effort so they did not bother. From these young women's perspectives, the few relatively positive personal exchanges with teachers were outweighed by the many confrontational and demeaning experiences at Burncoat Senior High.

When examining the factors that led to their achievement and engagement in middle school, the young women stressed that middle school was different. They felt cared for and supported and academically thrived in that setting. Their needs for relatedness and belonging were met by many adults within the school. In contrast, in secondary school they perceived themselves to be looked upon with disdain and instead of teachers and staff expecting the best, the worst was often anticipated. The transition from childhood to adolescence and from middle school to high school correlated with a change in relationship between students and school staff. These young women felt as if the staff no longer viewed them as students or individuals; rather they were perceived now as threats. This perception is extremely consequential for these adolescents as they have attributed their failures in high school as now uncontrollable, resulting in disengagement.

Communication with all the adults in their lives, including teachers, emerged as an impediment to their academic engagement and achievement. All of these young women expressed a strong desire to attend college after completing high school and were also the first generation in the family planning on attending college. Of great concern were their statements that no one within or outside of school had discussed college plans during their first two years of high school, including parents and counselors. The students reiterated on several occasions that no one was discussing college with them.

In informal discussions, the parents and guardians of these girls expressed that they discuss "school," including the prospect of college, on an average of two to three times per week. These statements clearly contradict student perceptions. That dichotomy can be explained. On re-interviewing students, it became clear that the young women did not receive practical answers to their questions regarding college, that is, prerequisites, application process, and so on. Rather they have received "talks" regarding college in a punitive, disciplinary approach in terms of what could be taken away, and the ruin their lives would be in if they did not apply themselves more to their education.

While the fears of parents who have not been to college are understandable, the same cannot be said for educators who attended and excelled at college. Even if conversations appear to be ineffective because they are inexperienced with college mechanics, the parents and guardians of these young women stated unwavering support for their daughters' academic endeavors. They also expressed their anger at the school for not helping the students achieve to their fullest potential. As one parent stated ". . . she can't let this school be her stopper."

Clearly, the parents as well as the students found the Burncoat climate to be unsupportive. The girls' statements are supported by the results from my student body survey. Only 53 percent of Burncoat students stated that a member of the Burncoat staff has spoken to them regarding future career options. Of more concern is that only 40 percent of Burncoat students report that any adult within the school has discussed college with them. For these conversations not to be happening in a meaningful way with 60 percent of the student body is extremely troubling. Failing to have these conversations limits a vulnerable population's access to information. A lack of practical information as well as informed concern puts such students even further behind more acculturated peers for post-secondary career and schooling options.

While the girls mentioned previously remained engaged on some level academically, attending school regularly, being involved in school clubs, sports and organizations, and completing academic assignments, many displayed oppositional behavior toward authority figures in the school, an early warning sign of disengagement. It appears that their affective engagement is being most impacted by their interpersonal relationships, specifically with school staff. Research indicates that both behavioral and affective engagement is negatively impacted by lack of teacher support (Cummins 1996; Hudley, et al. 2003). This is a variable teachers could change. At Burncoat, the afternoon discussion groups, and surveys that supplied my data, in themselves constituted a change that was startling, given how easy it was to introduce.

Two years after the initial groups were held a follow-up meeting was conducted. The young women presented themselves as strong, independent, confident students. While still facing academic challenges, the majority went from failing several subjects to solid B average students. In addition to a perceptible improvement in grade average a clear trend emerged. Transcripts made clear that the students who engaged in conversations about college two years before had taken on classes with more academic rigor. In the ninth and tenth grade, these students for the most part, were placed in Burncoat's two lowest academic levels. After the initial focus groups, the number of students in honors and college prep increased. By twelfth grade, none of the girls were taking the lowest academic level courses and two students had taken advanced placement courses.

The majority of the young women in the original focus group were graduating on time and planning on attending either junior college or career training programs. There were two deviations from this trend. Raquel wrapped up her academic career in an alternative program and Lissettee needed a few more credits for graduation. However, both of these girls also scored high in self-efficacy, meaning all of the girls in the study now believed they could impart change and succeed academically, personally, and socially.

While the participants reported greater academic challenges and rigor, the data shows their self-concept scores all increased or were consistent with earlier high scores. The general self-concept score remained stable at the forty-second percentile over the two year span, showing that while self-concept may remain stable, attribution may indeed be malleable.

Re-interviewing the student subjects also made clear that markers for healthy and unhealthy interpersonal relationships had showed a distinct shift to "healthy." Instead of using terms such as "degrading" and "disrespectful" to describe many of their teachers, they now used terms such as "sweetheart" and "friend." This is a transformative change in relationship that the students directly attribute to their increased attendance in class and desire to engage in learning. They took on the challenge of fully investing in their education and building relationships with school staff. Seven of the girls named female teachers and guidance counselors as someone who helps them out the most academically and who they can turn to for advice both academically and personally. In addition, these seven as well as another two also named mothers, sisters, and grandmothers as part of their micro-support network. Interestingly, none of the young women named a male teacher or male family member.

During our earliest focus groups, these students were exposed to information regarding social systems and the relationship to their position within these systems in an attempt to promote self-efficacy. Their attributions had now shifted from uncontrollable to controllable, and from external to internal; they now believed they had the power to transform their academic experience. This belief was reflected in how they approached their academic learning, relationships with school staff, and parents. Hopelessness was replaced with information and empowerment. In addition, it appears maturation played a role in the process of engagement for these students. There is a stark contrast in student perceptions of teachers from grade ten to grade twelve. These young ladies originally had a very concrete method of analyzing their teachers in grade ten, that is, they like you or they don't, they are racist or they are not, they either want me to succeed or they don't.

By grade twelve, the same students were not only able to view themselves in terms of their multiple identities as ethnic minority female students operating in a complex educational system and society; they were able to view their teachers in a similar light. They were able to see many of the teachers as also having multiple dimensions and the students began to recognize the constraints teachers face operating within the same complex systems. Thus, with this cognitive ability and insight students were able to let their guard down per se and by grade twelve the students were able to form bonds with some teachers at Burncoat. It would seem that the girls, in modifying their behavior, had modified the behavior of the adults in their lives. Adults should try the process in reverse rather than respond to students with preconceived notions of "good student behavior" the students have never been taught or motivated to learn.

SOME NECESSARY CONCLUSIONS

Much of the research conducted regarding student engagement and achievement centers on data drawn after students have become disengaged. That data focuses solely on casual explanations without itself "engaging" students in the discussion in a meaningful way. Utilizing focus groups, then leading students into critical thought and dialogue regarding social systems and their position within these systems should be the first step in any process reviewing the relationship of engagement to success. Supporting students as they begin to shift their attribution in relation to success and failure is, moreover, imperative to improving their self-efficacy, engagement, and achievement before any other remediation has begun. In other words, the very act of investigation has consequences and these should be maximized for positive outcome.

The students in this study exhibited early signs of disengagement; however, they were not fully disengaged from academics. They expressed disenchantment with the educational institution, educational process, and those in authority. At the same time, they also expressed interest and excitement regarding college, scholarships, and the future. At the end of the tenth grade year, they had improved upon their dismal ninth grade performance and had two full years to become fully engaged with the help of their parents and school staff. What we have learned about student engagement is that it is not an option if we want students to reach their fullest potential academically. Unfortunately, we also know upwards of one third of students in the United States are disengaged by the time they reach ninth grade (DeWit, Karioja, and Rye 2010). Race, socioeconomic status, and gender all have the potential to impact engagement, depending on the individual's level of resiliency. Disengagement is largely correlated with the transition out of elementary school settings. The elementary school experience is one that is ripe for developing close personal relationships between teachers and students due to the fact that students often stay in the same cohort and typically have the same teacher for at least one academic year. Young children are also not perceived as a threat by their teachers.

In Worcester, beginning in grade four, the curriculum moves toward departmentalization. That means students will typically have three teachers, one different for each subject: English language arts, social studies/science, and mathematics. By middle school the number of teachers each student sees grows and the amount of time the student spends with each teacher diminishes. Thus, the opportunity to develop interpersonal connections is reduced in both the student and teacher role. In addition, the movement between classes with various groupings of students, and the removal of recess by middle school, reduces peer-to-peer interactions. This is problematic for adolescents, as they are at a developmental stage where they are looking for independence from parental figures and looking for support from teachers and peers. The secondary system, unlike the elementary school level, no longer naturally affords and promotes relationships. Therefore, it takes concerted effort from both the teacher and student to build relationships, no small endeavor given the various challenges already being faced by both populations.

Educational researchers note that the relationship between student and teacher is paramount to achieving academic success. The push for highly qualified teachers through NCLB is commendable; nevertheless, failure to acknowledge the importance of relationships will limit the success that highly qualified teachers can achieve in the classroom (Shaunessy and McHatton 2009). The Burncoat student population was clearly bifurcated along ability groupings and race as it relates to perception regarding teachers:

> My teachers are awesome!
>
> I would like to say that I never have been this confident in any of my schools, as I am in Burncoat High School.
>
> I really do enjoy learning here and challenging my mental ability. I want to go far and get my doctorate.
>
> I love this school and the teachers in it!
>
> Entering high school was somewhat scary but once I entered into this mysterious hallow, I found myself oddly comfortable and relaxed. There are many teachers that I really learn from.
>
> This school has great teachers and they want you to pass.

The students quoted above were all honors and advanced placement level students. In particular, advanced placement students rained kudos upon the Burncoat staff and that is an achievement that teachers rightly cherish. Importantly, the ethnic background of students, although the majority of students were white, did not seem to factor in at the upper academic levels in regards to student teacher relationships. What was a factor? Early and sustained engagement.

> Dismiss all of the teachers and start over please.
>
> I don't like this school, it gives me no support.
>
> I know school is important because in today's society you need a good education to get a decent job. But I hate school because most teachers show very low interest in the feelings of the students, causing students to act out against each other.
>
> Why do you care? They don't.
>
> The teachers and school staff need to learn about EVERY student in order for them to succeed.
>
> I need to feel more involved, more connected. I wish we had the freedom to get involved in the school.
>
> We as students need better teachers that care encourage and support us.
>
> There are some teachers that don't care at all.

My motivation to go to school is myself and my best friends motivate me. Forget about the teachers.

Teachers need to be paid more so they will try harder.

Please make Burncoat High better.

The students who responded in this manner were ethnically diverse: primarily white, black, and Latino. Overwhelmingly, they were either in all college prep courses or a mix of college prep and honors. While disagreeing about the quality of teachers at Burncoat, the two groups of students—the satisfied and the dissatisfied—agreed that teachers respond differently to various students. Jose, a Latino student enrolled in college prep courses wrote, ". . . but I like the place, my teachers make me care, I'm grateful to be here. It's not the place, it's who you are. I'm human, you're human, respect." Here Jose points out what several of the students who love their teachers acknowledged: it didn't really matter what level you were in when it comes to teacher-student relationships. Rather, relationships were predicated on how much perceived investment the student displayed in front of the teacher. If teachers perceived students wanting a relationship, they often put forth extra effort with those students. However, if a student showed little desire to connect with teachers or academics, teachers were quick to write the student off and divest from their efforts to engage.

Of even more concern were students suggesting particular teachers were punitive and vindictive, held grudges, and penalized various student subgroups on a whim. This is problematic as 66 percent of Burncoat students reported being motivated by teacher encouragement and support, yet only 30 percent believed all of their teachers truly believe in them academically. On a positive note, 79 percent of students believed there is at least one adult at Burncoat who wants them to succeed, however this is proving to not be enough for many students at Burncoat Senior High.

GUIDANCE PLEASE

The guidance department ("guidance and adjustment counselors" at Burncoat Senior High), were also lauded by students who appreciated counselors that put forth every effort in helping students succeed. Nothing exemplified this more than their reaction to the death of beloved guidance counselor, Maxine Levy (wife of former Worcester mayor, Jordan Levy) in 2010. The Burncoat community was devastated and rallied together, enacting a scholarship fund in Levy's name.

The counselors within the guidance department, although understaffed, were praised for encouraging students to do better academically, reinforcing the concept that students were often "better people and students" than credited or displayed through their behavior. Sixty-three percent of students reported that it is a counselor at Burncoat Senior High that is their greatest support.

> Bridgett stated, "I stopped trying after middle school but Mrs. Dowd told me I'm better than this. I wanted to die, I was really considering it you know, but thanks to her I got on meds. She saved my life and doesn't even know it." This young lady had none of the warning signs of being at risk. She was white, middle class, part of the magnet, and in honors.
> Principal Foley acknowledged the need for counselors at Burncoat, "Jane (Mrs. Dowd) has a dramatic impact on all kinds of kids she's like our Mother Theresa we need that person in school."

The counselors at Burncoat are clearly needed; they have, however, the responsibility of interacting with the entire school population regardless of SES, ethnicity, or ability level, and the case illustrated above in particular magnifies the need for this interaction and the impact a guidance counselor can have on students. How much easier might the over-taxed counselor's role be were the students to come to them feeling already valued?

TEACHERS MATTER

As students discussed their relationships with teachers and counselors, the words "care" and "respect" were often used. The students at Burncoat typify what the research tells us about caring teachers. Caring teachers are those that are fair, communicate well with students, allow students to have input, and express sincere interest in their lives outside of the classroom (Shaunessy and McHatton 2009). Students at Burncoat do not hesitate in expressing vehement disdain for the teachers that show no interest in them, do not seem to know their names, refuse to make eye contact in the hallways, and peel out of the driveway when the day ends. They note that many of their teachers often refer to Burncoat, the neighborhood, and the city in an insulting manner. Some teachers, according to student reports, go so far as to say in class "That's why I don't live in Worcester." Some teachers, again according to surveyed students, have expressed their own disdain for the teaching profession and their own career choice, citing lack of pay and respect as some of the many reasons they do not like their jobs. The students find all of this talk extremely disrespectful to who they are both as community members and students. Angela writes, "If you don't like your job, and you don't like us quit, but don't ruin our lives." This disconnection between students and teachers is significantly detrimental; 50 percent of students who have said that they have considered dropping out of school cite teachers as the reason.

Neighborhood matters, SES matters, race matters, physical plant matters, curricular materials matter, however the teacher doesn't just matter. The teacher-student relationship is central to educating children. NCLB promotes the hiring of highly qualified teachers. The Worcester public schools want certified teachers who have passed Massachusetts teachers' tests. However, we cannot simply think of highly qualified teachers as those that possess content knowledge. Highly qualified teachers must have the skills to engage students. As human beings, we all possess biases, but how we choose to handle our bias separate those who are fair, those adults who are agents of change, from those that are discriminatory and oppressive. Highly qualified teachers must examine their own biases, beliefs, and preconceived notions about various populations before becoming teachers. They must work on themselves before working with other people's children. Children cannot afford to be guinea pigs as teachers work out their identities.

Highly qualified teachers must have the innate desire to work in a collaborative manner in order to educate all children that enter their classrooms. Highly qualified teachers must accept that although adolescents may physically resemble adults, the teacher is the adult role model, and as such cannot place the onus of building an educational relationship and partnership on the student. A highly qualified teacher, then, cannot simply be an individual who passes a test, has a bachelor's degree, and no criminal record. Those are minimal, objective qualifications. The students at Burncoat and the students in America's public schools deserve more. We can do better. Teachers who come into the system idealistic, moreover, must regularly receive the support they need to examine how the stresses of their jobs have undone their ideals. School counselors and teachers should work together to connect with all students. The process of academic transmission does not occur in a vacuum.

Coinciding with the shift from childhood to adolescence and middle to high school, there should be greater practical discussion with students regarding attributions and self-efficacy. This ongoing discussion should be emancipatory by design, encouraging change within the school system and society that will enable students to grow as students and individuals. State mandated exams and increases in academic requirements, as those exemplified in No Child Left Behind, may be beneficial to some students, however, careful attention and monetary resources should also be spent on mentorship, minority hiring, staff workshops and professional development; on building relationships within the school, as well as school-family partnerships, particularly in urban communities. These Burncoat students possess the academic self-concept to achieve. The roadblocks to their success lay in the interpersonal relationships with adults and the school climate.

While some students believe the recent leadership of Principal Foley and his administrative team, as well as the guidance department were moving the school in the right direction, there still appeared to be a strong disconnect between many staff members and the students at Burncoat. However, just as the students noted, and I would be remiss if I did not note that there are indeed some tremendous teachers at Burncoat, dedicating time, money, and most importantly emotional energy to the betterment of their students and the school community. Principal Foley, understanding the importance of relationship, established the "Focus on Freshmen" programmatic shift at Burncoat:

> If you talk to ninth grade kids versus the end of twelfth grade, they are more mature and have a greater perspective. To that point, we recognize the middle school transition. In a simply stated way I thought we needed to look at eighth grade and get the front end of grade nine to look more like the back end of grade eight and the back end of grade eight to look more like the front end of grade nine. So we developed a focus on freshmen to work on those personalized relationships. We took a cohort of eight to ten students and a staff member as an academic liaison and point person to communicate between home and school; they had one on one parent conferences by phone or in person. We had sixty families in. For that period of time that followed, there was some improvement. We are doing a better job recognizing the need of greater personalization in grade nine. Twelfth grade students have a different perspective on their role in their own education. (Principal Foley)

Many Burncoat teachers should be acknowledged for battling what at times seem to be, and quite frankly are, inconceivable hurdles placed in the way of educating students. Principal Foley, Mrs. Dowd, and several other teachers at Burncoat are also graduates of the school; they along with staff that instantly fell in love with this diverse, exciting community indeed bleed green (the school color). The hours these teachers put into bonding with their students through coaching, mentoring, attending school events on their own time, and most importantly through teaching, cannot be sufficiently rewarded. The pride they feel for their school and students most assuredly has a positive impact on the students as well. However, even these dedicated and driven teachers are at times physically and emotionally drained; they are on the front lines often without the manpower and weapons to win the battle. They are too often working alongside colleagues who have divested.

We must assume that no one enters the teaching profession with the idea of destroying children, or to get rich, or for some miss-perceived ease of the profession. We must assume neither did the teachers that Burncoat students identify as racist or as hating their jobs. They did not join this profession to discriminate against children of various ethnic backgrounds. Nor did these teachers choose to join this profession in order to spend their days hating their job. Teachers are human, a fact ninth graders may not recognize but that twelfth graders, with good interpersonal relationships with their teachers, do come to understand. And yes, teachers are severely impacted by the stress associated with the current state of public education in America. The shifting demographics, lack of resources, differing city, state, and federal standards, and the increasing social and psychological needs of the adolescent population they work with all contribute to the mounting stress and frustration being experienced by teachers in urban America. Those who should be advocating for teachers, however, are too often caught up in their own intellectual and emotional investment in what they believe, rather than know, is "best."

That division can also be seen in paradigmatic Worcester as external administrators dictate standards and responses. As the pressures mount within Burncoat in relation to meeting NCLB requirements, Burncoat Senior High inches ever so closer to being identified as a level four school; the staff is splitting within their own ranks. The level four designation would require restructuring of the school, and could include the removal of the principal and some staff as well as introduce sweeping changes in the curriculum. Principal Foley and his team work at a fevered pitch to stave off this label, instituting remedial help, drop-out prevention programs, MCAS tutoring, and social service programs such as having a food pantry on site. Yet Foley is also getting push back from some of his own staff. Unhappy with the extra work survival may entail, with little to no extra compensation in sight, some Burncoat High teachers are refusing to cooperate with Principal Foley's agenda, making his job as an urban principal all the more difficult. Based on the student perspective, we can see there is also a definitive split between the teachers who comprehend the diversity of Burncoat as a treasure and those that find that diversity detrimental. Principal Foley, despite the best intentions, has been unable to rally his staff or unite them with the common goal of success for all. His plight is that of the good American urban school principal.

What is transpiring at Burncoat is also being replicated on the district level. While Superintendent Boone, many of her administrators, and various instructional coaches, are energized regarding academic initiatives, they are having difficulty when it comes to motivating and unifying staff ranks in the school district. As elsewhere, the Worcester teacher's union is a strong force. Much like many organizations with a unionized workforce, the union's agenda is often in opposition to that of leadership. Or at the very least, the two force visions for resolving crises or putting agenda into practice are on two different planes.

Worcester's school committee, charged with bridging the gap between community and the school system, is often at odds with their own governing body. In addition, much of the rhetoric on controversial issues tends to attack or show disrespect, on any given day, for community groups or the superintendent herself. The rhetoric during school committee meetings, in teacher's lounges, in the local newspaper, on blogs, and among parents waiting at the bus stop ranges from attacks on policy to personal attacks on individuals as well as on whole ethnic and socioeconomic communities. These various stakeholders—from parents to educational professionals within the system— feel they have everything to lose if the educational system continues in the direction that it is headed. But instead of uniting, stakeholders have invoked rhetoric that has become increasingly personal, uncivil, and separatist in nature.

I asked Superintendent Boone how she deals with the various stakeholders. Remember, she came into this system as an often unwanted outsider. She had to tread lightly. Dr. Boone, a woman of deep faith, responded to my question:

> The first part of that question is my faith. If you lead to survive you do everything someone wants you to do. If you lead to succeed you do the right things for the right reason. You will bump up against peoples' beliefs and values. I'm not worried about tomorrow. My job is hard. It should not be as difficult as it is. It's hard to get the powers that be to really focus on children. The attacks have been very personal. I represent the face of what a lot of people didn't want to deal with, change. If we always run to where it is comfortable how do we impact change? What I've had to do is figure out how do I navigate the political context? So the best way is to do it through student perspective and to have authentic relationships. Then that will survive long after I'm gone because the parents will never disengage from authentic community they will have a real voice. And so it's amazing, civil rights issues are as alive today as they were in the sixties. The methodology that we use to address them can't be the same, sit-ins, riots, but now we have to have a much more intellectual, strategic battle. Hopefully what I'm demonstrating, I think I'm doing what God expects me to do, but if I join the fight they want me to join then I'm no better than they are. I don't give the community any sense of hope if I join a lowly fight. I need to know how to build networks and coalitions, know your subject and have a logical argument. I make it about the kids because I'm here for a season, whatever that is, when I leave I don't want the work to have been about me. I want the work to have been around the children. So that people won't disengage from the work. Whenever my season is up, part of the work God wants me to do is to wake up the community to see that there is hope for them, even when others have told them there is none. While the tension is a big part of my leadership, do we exist (public education) for the adults or for the students? Stop fighting each other, at some point it has got to be about the children. (Superintendent Boone)

The conversation regarding education in Worcester, similar to those taking place in other urban districts, has become one about the adults, not a dialogue about the children. Union rights, teacher's rights, parent's rights, the rights of the poor, people of color, the marginalized, teachers, principals, the superintendent, the government have been set against each other. The children, especially those caught at that awkward age we call adolescence cannot be heard in the din of voices.

The lessons of this study inevitably point to one truth: everyone in the urban public school, from the superintendent to the teacher to the staff to the student, is at-risk, yet hold great promise. Across America's urban landscape, the tenure of superintendents and principals can often be counted in months rather than years; the average burn-out rate for teachers is three to five years. Clearly, attitudinal and behavioral shifts by all members of the school community must become part of the macro educational plan to build, retain, and nurture a true educational community. Resiliency, once a concern we had about the children, must be fostered in students and staff alike. And adults must lead the way.

Chapter 6

The Fight for Survival

What our city is today is due largely to the schools of the past, so what it
will be in the future will depend upon the character and standard of the
schools which we maintain.

—1902 Mayoral Inaugural Address Worcester, Massachusetts

The United States, and Worcester, Massachusetts, as a microcosm of the
whole, was built in large part by immigrants. Historians have documented
the many trials and tribulations faced by each immigrant group as they sought
to make new homes and new lives in America. However, our current sociohistoric context gives one pause when exploring how equipped the United
States is to deal with the remarkable diversity within its borders. Given the
shifting demographics in the United States and current educational data, it is
increasingly apparent that the country was not prepared to deal with the dramatic shift in demographics that has impacted public schooling. And so the
question emerges: Can public schools survive the changing face of America? I
posed this question to the leader of the Worcester public schools, Dr. Melinda
Boone, and to the leader of Burncoat Senior High, Principal William Foley.

Yes, public schools have to survive. Trite, but education is the great equalizer so
you will always have to provide kids with public education. The federal, state,
district level is over there. What we have to focus on is here. I tell my staff you
guys worry about what is happening in these four walls inside these classrooms,
we're going to do the best for these kids. I'll worry about that, and we'll let them
worry about the big stuff. We'll do our best, we'll continue to do a better job,
we'll put more kids in AP. We'll do what we can here, without necessarily feeling like it's an overwhelming burden. We need to be narrowly focused on the
local level. The politics aren't about kids. There are people in this area whose

families have always been in this area who will always be in this area. We're the best option around, better than many of the parochial options. But if we can begin to get past parents worried about kids being safe we're going to stem the tide of students going to private schools or school choice. It's just; I really do believe that we are making good strides. It will continue to take a commitment on the part of the adults. We need to produce a better prepared kid. There are a lot of political decisions made by non-education professionals that aren't in the best interest of kids. We can't just have the magnet. We need programs for the other kids. The budget cuts have cut back on options that kids have available. We have our JROTC program; it grabs a lot of kids to build community. We now have a connection between us and Quinsigamond Community College in our auto tech program another good option. Our avid program is introducing kids to experiences on college campuses that they might not otherwise have. We have to be creative and find different ways to engage kids other than the standard. (Principal Foley)

I agree standards themselves and accountability have not doomed public educa-tion. I equate it to post *Brown vs. Board of Education*. It said equal access but it didn't create equal outcomes. As a country we have to own that. Political rhetoric aside, No Child Left Behind created a conversation in this nation that all children should have comparable access for outcomes so how do we help that? I think the problem in No Child Left Behind is that it was too focused on student accountability and had very little adult accountability. The way it was established allowed adults to hide behind student demographics and challenges, teachers believe "well we've done the best we can if the student is a senior in high school had pre-k my job would have been easier they would have been successful." That's a fairy tale story. I think under the Obama administration, the pendulum did shift and we have some adult accountability. But I think we've gone too far that we've traded student accountability for adult accountability and we're out of balance again. I worry about the perceived silver bullet. I've said to people, there's so much that can happen here. You know I respect what has gone before me and I know the value of public education and it can still be done right. But we have to have mutual respect for the families and students who are attending the public schools. The question is do we have the will to do it? We know how to do it, and that's why I spend my best time every month with my student advisory committee. What they (students) are saying makes a great deal of sense. But when we sit there and think about decisions that we make sometimes . . . I got to fight the fight because it is the right thing, it is the right thing and you know I'm not going to sit here and act like I'm not fighting for kids. I think public education can survive, but it has to survive from the inside. We have to be willing to make the changes, to hold fast to what we know is making a difference and be able to document that well, to be able to push our own thinking as to what access means. (Superintendent Boone)

The question may be better stated as: In what form does American pub-lic education survive? In order for public schooling in the United States to survive, specifically urban schools, we must work on building resiliency and community. As Principal Foley stated it will take a concerted effort on the part of all stakeholders. Dr. Boone often begins many of her presentations with an image of a child and clearly articulates the need for all decisions to be based on the child. How do we stop the contentious battle between haves and have nots, between policymakers and practitioners, between unions and administration?

BUILDING RESILIENCE

As stakeholders we must drop our weapons and focus on the children. We must stop making this process of education about adults. Thus with the child in mind and with the complete and realistic perspective that educational stakeholders cannot solve all of societal ills in one clean sweep, we must examine how we as adults can build educational resiliency within students and create resilient schools. The first step in this process is to view all students and schools as holding promise rather than being at risk. A model proposed by Benard and Marshall (1997) holds value when examining resilience (see Figure 6.1).

While resilience can be encouraged and nurtured, the model proposed by Benard and Marshall suggests a methodology for tapping natural resilience in individuals. Beginning with the concept of belief, many urban students as indicated by Burncoat's student population recognize that their teachers do not believe in them as students. The rhetoric regarding the state of urban

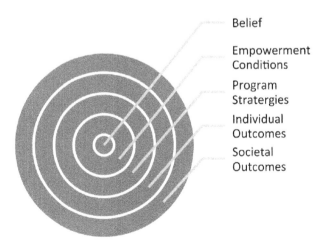

Belief

Empowerment
Conditions

Program
Stratergies

Individual
Outcomes

Societal
Outcomes

Figure 6.1 Framework for Tapping Resiliency. *Source*: Adapted from Benard and Marshall 1997.

education in America is very public. The rhetoric and behavior regarding expectations and beliefs inside the walls of urban high schools is also readily accessible to students and they digest every morsel. In order to promote resilience and thus lead to eventual higher achievement we must start at the very beginning, with the two groups that have the most impact on a students' life both within schools and at home. Families and teachers are, and have always been, pivotal in shaping educational outcomes for students. However, these two stakeholder groups cannot be successful in isolation. Although frustrating for many educators the needs of America's changing student population, indeed the economic and familial changes on a societal level, indicate a great need for change in how we approach education in the twenty-first century.

BELIEVING

Teachers cannot effectively do their job of educating students if they hold firm to the model that their sole responsibility is to transmit academic content knowledge. The whole child must be educated and nurtured, this cannot end in sixth grade, the nurturing must continue through secondary school. The complexity of American society has in turn created the twenty-first-century student who is complex as well. At Burncoat this means the staff has had to adapt, and many have tried, however only some have been successful. Teachers become mentors as well as pseudo-counselors. Counselors take on more students, work longer hours, and work collaboratively to not only help students but educate the faculty as well. Administrators approve programs both academic, such as the focus on freshman, and need-based, such as the food pantry at Burncoat. For many adults in the halls and classrooms of Burncoat acceptance of where American public education stands and what America's students need has long passed and they are dedicated to meeting the great demand with the limited resources at their disposal. For these dedicated educators, belief is there, they view Burncoat students as having great promise and unique talents rather than seeing them as only at-risk. These educators fight for the survival of their students, of their school, and the survival of urban education. However, in every educational institution there are individuals who do not believe in students.

In the twenty-first century teachers are under attack in ways that have never been seen before in American public education. Teaching methodologies and commitment being questioned at every turn while more effort, time, and personal resources are being asked of them with no additional compensation or respect given in return. I venture an educated guess that if some of the same questions regarding self-concept, school climate, and so on were posed to the faculty at Burncoat similar issues would rise to the top, respect, academic effort, community. For those that have divested and do not believe in their student body's ability to achieve one can ascribe generalizations of racism, or classism as casual factors. However, to do so would limit the responsibility of the various stakeholders and partners in education. The unrelenting professional pressures and dramatic demographic shifts in public education over the last thirty years have impacted our aging teaching force. For many of these teachers and administrators throughout America adapting to the demographic shifts in and of themselves would have been an issue that required diligence, effort, and creative thinking. However, with the NCLB legislation, over the past ten years what once would have been an arduous challenge became for many educators an insurmountable battle that they resigned to losing. That being said it does not excuse educators from educating; it does not absolve teachers from focusing on all children regardless of ethnicity and socioeconomic status. America literally cannot afford to throw away students. To push students out into the workforce without the proper education is not only contributing to the failure of these children but to the failure of American society. What the current educational context clearly indicates is the requisite need to not only work on resiliency for students but for educators as well. Those educators that have divested have thrown in the towel and are not resilient themselves. Seldom are America's teachers lauded or heralded for their diligence and commitment. Rather the default assumption is that to be a teacher is an easy job, requires little effort, and affords individuals countless days and hours of downtime. This rather ignorant rhetoric has been digested by many divested educators; they have been worn down by the sheer lack of support.

To have true resilience for America's students, we must have resilient teachers. Someone needs to believe in them. The powerful collaboration of teachers who have self-efficacy and the belief that they are still, regardless of changes in society and legislation, instrumental in the development of every student that sits before them, and students who regardless of personal circumstances believe they can be successful academically and contributing members of society is a force so powerful that it truly can combat the effects of race and poverty. Teachers must overcome the pressures that have become detrimental to their ability to teach and get back to viewing students as students rather than impediments to their livelihood.

Family and community also play a pivotal role in supporting students and teachers. Regardless of ethnicity and socioeconomic status families and community members need to behave as role models as it pertains to educational expectations and relationships. If the goal is higher achievement and educational attainment for students families must set high academic expectations. Completion of educational benchmarks should be conveyed to students as mandatory not optional. For example, high achieving students at Burncoat often expressed this notion with the example of college expectations. As their families often discussed college attendance as a given not a choice, using vocabulary such as "when you go to college" rather than "if you go to college." Attending school regularly, time on homework, and enrichment activities should be reinforced as priorities, not options. Families and community members, regardless of educational background or socioeconomic status have the capacity to show respect and excitement toward education as the key to upward mobility and access to lifelong career options. In addition, families and community members have the great responsibility of showing mutual respect for teachers and school administration.

The relationship between families and community and teachers and administrators is paramount in achieving a healthy holistic education for students. For the adults within a student's microsystem to be at odds with one another creates hostility that will permeate the educational experience. Much like parents who argue behind closed doors, or divorced parents who never speak, children are keenly aware of relational strife amongst the adults in their world, educators are no exception, and this strife is impactful with both short term and long-term consequences for the student. Therefore, it is the responsibility of adults in this microsystem, to display, and reinforce healthy, respectful communication, and to work together toward the best interest of the student.

Families and communities, particularly ethnic minority communities, also have an important role in shaping who will teach the next generation. Too often, when motivated and academically talented ethnic minority students show an interest in becoming a teacher they are discouraged by family and redirected to a more lucrative career. This is due largely in part to families wanting motivated students to be as successful as possible. However, it is yet one more way the message is being conveyed that teachers are not valuable to our society. Members of various ethnic groups and social classes, as well as the students at Burncoat lament the fact that they are not justly represented amongst the teaching ranks. Some of the onus must fall back on the community; the responsibility cannot simply rest in human resources. The community should express to students k–12, and those of college age, that one of the most important contributors to society are teachers as they shape thousands of children during their careers. Showing respect for the vocation and encouraging educated and successful members of the community to become teachers will have an impact on the teaching force for future generations.

Ultimately, to begin the journey toward academic achievement students and teachers must believe in themselves. They must have self-efficacy, the belief that they can accomplish goals. Various stakeholders including administration, unions, the school community, families, and the entire community

will need to work together in order to support the development and maintenance of self-efficacy within the school community.

EMPOWERING CONDITIONS

For some of these educators belief has turned directly into programmatic
strategies. However, referring to the model on tapping natural resilience there
is a step that is too often ignored. Indeed, schools that skip the empowerment
conditions stage do so at their own peril. The nucleus of the educational system should be the student. If the student is not being educated in a system
that empowers them as individuals, resilience and academic success becomes
a mere faded dream. If the student has adults in their lives who convey belief
in their abilities yet attend a school that does not empower them, reaching full
potential will be extremely difficult.

Empowering conditions are varied as they relate to the school environment. Whole school conditions include providing a safe and nurturing environment. There is a fine line between keeping students safe and operating
urban schools as prison-like facilities. Security guards, police presence, metal
detectors, and zero tolerance policies may be successful in conveying a serious hard line position on violence in schools to the general public. However,
it also can send a stigmatizing message to those educators and students within
the school. As Principal Foley noted, safety is one reason families opt out of
urban schools. Burncoat like the majority of schools in urban America is safe.
The stigma, stereotypes, and misconceptions regarding urban living, and in
particular the changing face of America's urban residents, leave many with
the feeling of being unsafe. America's urban students often share similar feelings. How safe students feel will largely be predicated on how they are treated
within their school and how school staff manage deviant behavior. Thus, in
order for students to feel safe within their school the school staff must also
feel safe and view students as non-threatening. Once this rudimentary step
towards empowering conditions has been fulfilled there are multiple factors
controlled by various stakeholders that must come together in order to truly
have a school that empowers students and staff.

The first is the condition of the physical plant. Jonathan Kozol has done a
remarkable job of documenting the conditions of America's urban schools.
For example, attending schools that do not have functioning restrooms or
toiletries within restrooms, antiquated heating systems where temperatures
vary by double digits between classrooms, rusty walls, peeled paint, lifted
floor tiles that may or may not contain carcinogens, does not afford either the
student or teacher a modicum of comfort in which to educate or be educated.
In the world of education students and parents often follow the shiny new

building. The building in and of itself does not make for a better education. It is the relationships within the building that empower students. However, the physical plant, structure and condition of the school, can serve to promote the esteem of students and teachers, as well as investment from parents. A school in good condition garners respect and pride from those who attend. A school in disrepair can lead to embarrassment, lack of respect for the school, and a diminished connection to the school community. Therefore, the condition of the physical plant has some indirect impact on student achievement. Thus, even in trying economic times care should be taken in maintaining or renovating deteriorating school buildings.

In order to provide empowering conditions for students and staff proper resources must also be available. In high schools across America, and in Worcester, Massachusetts, students do not have enough of the basic tools to receive a proper education such as textbooks. Many secondary students are unable to bring textbooks home because they are being shared amongst classes. The supply list given to parents at the beginning of the school year now often includes reams of copy paper and dry erase markers because the school does not have the monetary resources to provide for teachers or students. Teachers spend hundreds of dollars on their own in order to conduct basic classroom lessons. The technology seen on college campuses and in many private homes has often skipped the urban classroom where outdated technology is the only technological resource on hand for students and teachers alike. Without educational resources the roles of student and teacher become all the more challenging.

While there are many factors that contribute to empowering conditions within a school the last I will mention is the building and nurturing of community. An empowering school community is one in which diversity is welcomed and respected. Interaction between students and staff transcends ethnicity and socioeconomic class. In order to foster community building, school staff must be willing and able to interrupt instances of prejudice, discrimination, and segregation within the school. Student leaders must also rise to the challenge and interrupt negative and disruptive behaviors that have the potential to dismantle the school community. The discussion of neighborhood and relationships in the previous chapters can be looked to for inspiration as to how students and teachers can impact school community. Just as certain neighborhoods provide social capital for students a healthy school community can do the same. In productive, healthy school communities, relationships will be nurtured, and high social and academic expectations will become normative. Community is not a concept that can be built by regulations, rather it must come from those living within the school walls, thus, the two stakeholders at the center of education, teachers and students, have an obligation to build a healthy community.

PROGRAMMATIC STRATEGIES AND OUTCOMES

A myriad of programmatic strategies to improve resilience and achievement can be found in literature and in every school district across America. Burncoat exemplifies this with Principal Foley's Focus on Freshmen program designed to improve community and achievement in the ninth grade. The Worcester School District adopted programmatic shifts to improve the academic rigor of the various academic tracks. However, these programs were often being implemented without the two foundational levels outlined above. Just as a house with no foundation will crumble, placing programmatic changes atop disillusioned and divested students and teachers who are navigating a hostile educational environment will surely result in programmatic failure. Therefore, the foundation must be built first although some social programmatic strategies that reinforce and build empowerment conditions can occur concurrently with academic programmatic strategies.

Academic programmatic strategies should relate to several of the dimensions outlined by James Banks (2006). While Banks articulates strategies as they pertain to multicultural education several overarching themes emerge that are imperative to the transformation of American urban education. The first dimension is An Equity Pedagogy. This, amongst educators is often referred to as differentiated instruction. Programmatic strategies in this arena should focus on pedagogy. Teachers should be encouraged to take into account the differences, both intellectual and cultural, amongst students and modify instruction accordingly. While simplistic in theory, the time teachers will need to alter lesson plans, attend professional development training, and modify instructional techniques may be daunting and somewhat intimidating. The various stakeholders should support and encourage this transformation with monetary resources and policy shifts when necessary. Teachers must be willing to participate in this transformation as well; forced participation in this programmatic shift will only serve to alienate teachers further and cause additional hostility between educational stakeholders. Therefore, it is clear that once again stakeholders must come together to facilitate these programmatic shifts.

Two additional multicultural education dimensions that can be adapted from Banks include Content Integration and the Knowledge Construction Process. While Banks encourages curricular content integration that includes examples and content across cultures. In order for content integration to be truly beneficial and aid in developing resilience, programmatic strategies should include problem and project based learning as well as curricular content that connects to students lives post-secondary years. Without a connection to the future students faced with various challenges may wallow in their current context unable to conjure up future possibilities. This then relates to the knowledge construction process. As outlined in the previous chapters students are remarkable and are capable of negotiating their educational context given the proper tools. Programmatic strategies that pertain to the knowledge construction process would encourage students to examine their own thinking, emphasizing the metacognitive process. These programmatic strategies should include critical thinking skills as it relates to curricular content and as it relates to students own assumptions and perspectives. Therefore, students should be encouraged to think critically about their own thought processes. While teachers are adopting equity pedagogy, students, as stakeholders in their own education, must critically reflect on how they perceive information, as well as how they view their educational process in totality. Students, teachers, and other stakeholders, will then be able to work collaboratively to support positive contributing factors while shifting negative factors that impact resilience and achievement. These are brief examples of overarching programmatic themes that could be utilized to improve resilience and achievement.

Given the model outlined, a solid base would be established wherein educational stakeholders believe that all children that attend America's public schools have promise and hold inherent talents. These promising students, in opposition to at-risk students, would then attend schools that have the social and structural conditions in which to empower all students. Within this empowering educational facility academic programmatic strategies would be implemented on a continuous basis in order to support resilience and achievement. Ultimately this dedication of stakeholders will bear the fruit of individual student resilience and achievement outcomes. When nourished and replicated this fruit will multiply consequently producing positive societal shifts and outcomes.

To revisit the question and subsequent answer on public school survival, the answer is yes, public school can survive. However, what is abundantly clear is that it cannot survive in a healthy form while clinging to an antiquated, nostalgic ideal of American society. The United States is diverse, it is not a melting pot, and while assimilation may happen to a certain extent it never occurs to the point that all children can be educated with the same cookie cutter approach. Horace Mann noted in 1839 that without the proper teacher training and support, as well as attention to the public school system public schools would become facilities for "charity" cases. Without dedication from all educational stakeholders Horace Mann's words could ring true well before the end of the twenty-first century.

There are notable patterns in school choice in urban centers. Many families unhappy with their local urban school choice opt for the free charter and magnet programs within their public school district. Those still unsatisfied will opt for the parochial school as this affords families a semblance of private education at a lower cost. Finally, those with the financial means often turn to private schools that often cost as much as college tuition. This flight pattern from urban public schools may be the direct consequence of America's inability to fully support public education further complicated by the stereotypes associated with the changing face of urban America. Thus, Mann in the end may be proven correct as America's urban public comprehensive high schools become the charity houses for the marginalized: the poor, the immigrants, and the special education students. If this transformation would come to fruition the current division between the haves and have nots in America will be seen as a crevice compared to the crater that would separate these two populations if urban public education were to succumb to its many challenges.

CONCLUSION

The trajectory of educational development in Worcester, Massachusetts, exemplifies the vast array of challenges faced by a growing American urban center. The dilemmas of the 1700 and 1800s as to whom should be educated, how they should be educated, and who should pay for said education are threads that weave in and out of the tapestry of educational debates for the next three hundred years. The twenty-first century brought the call to action and transformation through No Child Left Behind legislation, the unintended consequence being more children, teachers, and schools labeled as at-risk. Burncoat Senior High is a case study in urban education, a school community treading water in a desperate attempt to stay afloat in a sea of educational reform and fiscal crisis. Educational stakeholders are at odds, quite understandable when everything they hold dear is at risk. However, this dooms all involved to underachievement.

We must shift educational paradigms and build resilience in order to have true academic achievement for all. Educational reform and initiatives will not be successful when they are simply power grabs. Stakeholders must drop their weapons and agendas and focus on the nucleus, the student. Interpersonal relationships are the first step in the process of reforming our urban schools. In a society inundated by technology interpersonal communication has suffered tremendously. Relationships are the key and cornerstone to staving off school violence, bullying, and a plethora of socioemotional crises. Healthy relationships have the ability to assist all students—the popular, average, controversial, neglected, and rejected. Adult stakeholders have the power to model healthy relationships for students, through collaboration and compromise. In order to maintain creditability and usefulness, teachers unions, school committees, and school administration must look toward policy that positively impacts students, recognizing that whatever benefits the nucleus will eventually benefit the whole. However, these stakeholders cannot function in isolation. Families and communities must take on a prominent role in the education of children. Socioeconomic status, educational attainment, and ethnicity are not legitimate reasons to excuse participation. Educational professionals must respect that all family and community members have value around the table and should readily offer these constituents a seat. Finally state and federal government must allocate the appropriate resources to fund education.

Without a significant improvement of its urban education system, American students, and consequently American society, will have a precipitous drop in achievement. The American dream and success story will become an anomaly while we have the potential to make these stories the norm. Children are often voiceless in the debate on education therefore stakeholders must place personal and professional agendas on the backburner for the sake of our most vulnerable population. This is not the plight of the underserved, the poor, the marginalized, and the oppressed. This is the American story, how all stakeholders choose to respond will determine what American society shall be and how the rest of the story will be written.

References

ABC News. *ABC News: Good Morning America.* January 26, 2011. abcnews.go.com /US/ohio-mom-jailed-sending-kids-school-district/story?id=12763654 (accessed January 27, 2011).

Adams, Jane. "4 City Schools to Post Guards." *Telegram and Gazette,* July 20, 1990: A2.

Aikens, Nikki L., and Oscar Barbarin. "Socioeconomic Differences in Reading Trajectories: The Contribution of Family, Neighborhood, and School Contexts." *Journal of Educational Psychology,* 2008: 235–51.

Ainsworth, James W. "Why Does It Take a Village? The Mediation of Neighborhood Effects on Educational Achievement." *Social Forces,* 2002: 117–52.

Ainsworth-Darnell, James W., and Douglas B. Downey. "Assesing the Oppostional Culture Explanation for Racial/Ethnic Differences in School Performance." *American Sociological Review,* 1998: 536–53.

Allan, Susan. "Ability Grouping Research Reviews: What Do They Say about Grouping and the Gifted?" *Educational Leadership,* 1991: 60–65.

Ansalone, George. *Exploring Unequal Achievement in Schools.* New York: Lexington Books, 2009.

———. "Tracking, Schooling and the Equality of Educational Opportunity." *Race, Gender and Class,* 2009: 174–84.

Astell, Emilie. "Health Center Grows at GBV." *Telegram and Gazatte,* July 28, 1998: B1.

Auwarter, Amy E., and Mara S. Aruguete. "Effects of Student Gender and Socioeconomic Status on Teacher Perceptions." *The Journal of Educational Research,* 2008: 243–46.

Bailey, Deryl, and Pamela O. Paisley. "Nurturing and Decloping Excellence in Adolescent African American Males." *Journal of Counseling and Development,* 2004: 10–17.

Banks, James A. *Cultural Diversity and Education: Foundations, Curriculum, and Teaching.* Boston: Allyn & Bacon, 2006.

Barnard, Henry. "Normal Schools." 196. Carlisle, MA: Applewood Books, 1851.

Bernstein, Leonard. "GBV Neighbors Mourn Young Man's Death." *Sunday Telegram,* June 24, 1979.

Berzin, Stephanie C. "Educational Aspirations Among Low-Income Youths: Examining Multiple Conceptual Models." *Children and Schools*, 2010: 112–24.

Blezard, Robert. "Transfer Approved to Fund Nursery." *Evening Gazette*, January 17, 1986: 1, 2.

Bliss, Robert R. "ALPA Calls Survey An Insult." *Evening Gazette*, June 6, 1979: 25, 26.

———. "GBV Troubles Termed Inevitable." *Evening Gazette*, May 29, 1979: 1, 2.

———. "GBV-Some Changes a Year After Shooting." *Evening Gazette*, June 11, 1980: 25.

———. "Housing Authority Poll Shows Police Support." *Evening Gazette*, June 5, 1979: 1, 2.

———. "Project Residents Air Gripes." *Evening Gazette*, June 13, 1979: 25–26.

———. "Racial Balance Plan Proposed for 3 Housing Developments." *Evening Gazette*, December 12, 1979: 23–24.

———. "Seminars Aim to Ease Community Troubles." *Evening Gazette*, June 30, 1979: 1–2.

———. "Tenant Association Gets a Fesh Start." *Evening Gazette*, April 14, 1981: 13.

Bliss, Robert, and Mel Singer. "City Police Given GBV Beat." *Worcester Telegram*, June 21, 1979: 1, 2.

Blunt Jr., Roscoe C. "GBV Disturbance Injures 1;3 Held." *Evening Gazette*, July 22, 1975: 1.

———. "Housing Project Officer Charged With Murder." *Evening Gazette*, June 21, 1979: 1.

———. "Police to Boost Patrols at Troubled Projects." *Evening Gazette*, June 22, 1979: 1–2.

———. "Two Held Seven Hurt in GBV Disturbance." *Evening Gazette*, May 29, 1979: 1, 2.

Bourdieu, Pierre, and Loic Wacquant. *An Invitation to Reflexive Sociology.* Chicago: University of Chicago Press, 1992.

Bowles, Samuel, and Herbert Gintis. *Schooling in Capitalistic America.* New York: Basic Books, 1976.

Brody, Gene H, et al. "The Influence of Neighborhood Disadvantage, Collective Socialization, and Parenting on African American Children's Affiliation with Deviant Peers." *Child Development*, 2001: 1231–46.

Brofenbrenner, Urie, and Pamela Morris. "The Bioecological Model of Human Development." In *Theoretical Models of Human Development. Vol. 1 of the Handbook of Child Psychology (5th ed.)*, edited by Richard Lerner and William Damon, 793–828. New York: Wile, 2006.

Browning, Christopher, Tama Leventhal, and Jeanne Brooks-Gunn. "Sexual Initiation in Early Adolescence: The Nexus of Parental and Community Control." *American Sociological Review*, 2005: 758–78.

Bryant, Alison, and Marc Zimmerman. "Role Models and Psychosocial Outcomes among African American Adolescents." *Journal of Adolescent Research*, 2003: 36–67.

Bushnell, David. "GBV Police Rebute Hispanics' Charges." *Worcester Telegram*, February 15, 1979: 3, 15.

————. "WHA Police Officer Charged in Slaying." *Worcester Telegram*, June 22, 1979: 1, 12.

Bushnell, David, and Ernest Gallagher. "GBV Residents Claim Harrassment." *Worcester Telegram*, May 3, 1979: 1, 9.

Cammarota, Julio. "Disappearing in the Houdini Education." *Multicultural Education*, 2006: 2–10.

Central Massachusetts Regional Planning Commission. *Population studies for the Central Massachusetts Regional Planning District*. Worcester: Central Massachusetts Regional Planning Commission, 1967.

City of Worcester. 2012. www.worcesterma.gov/about-us (accessed January 5, 2012).

Collier, Geraldine A. "Facts, Figures are Clues to Future." *Evening Gazette*, September 25, 1986: 7.

————. "Drug War Manuevers at GBV." *Telegram and Gazette*, November 19, 1989: B1.

———— "Facts, Figures are Clues to the Future." *Evening Gazette*, September 25, 1986: 5.

————. "Racial Imbalance Growing in City Housing Projects." *Evening Gazette*, July 12, 1988: 1, 10.

————. "Healthy Commitments." *Telegram and Gazette*, February 1, 1993: C1–C2.

————. "WHA Receives Drug Grant." *Telegram and Gazette*, September 22, 1990: 3.

Commission on the Reorganization of Secondary Education. *The Cardinal Principles of Secondary Education*. Washington, DC: National Education Association, 1918.

Commonwealth vs. Hiram Estremera. 383 Mass. 382 (Worcester County, February 3, 1981).

Conchas, Gilberto. "Structuring Failure and Success: Understanding the Variability in Latino School Engagement." *Harvard Educational Review*, 2001: 475–505.

Connole, Dennia. *The Indians of Nipmuck Country in Southern New England, 1630–1750: An Historic Geography*. Jefferson, NC: McFarland & Company, Inc., 2001.

Connolly, Timothy J. "Burncoat Class of 66 Recalls Innocent Time." *Telegram and Gazette*, November 30, 1991: 3.

Conty, Edward J., and Leonard Bernstein. "Great Brook Valley Relatively Calm." *Worcester Telegram*, June 23, 1979: 5.

Courneyer, Edward, Bill Barry, Ernest Gallagher, Russel Eames, Scott Campbell, and David Bushell. "GBV Violence Follows Slaying." *Worcester Telegram*, June 22, 1979: 1, 12.

Cremin, Lawrence A., ed. *The Republic and the School: Horace Mann on the Education of Free Men*. New York: Teachers College, 1957.

Croteau, Scott J. "Burncoat High Locked Down; Threatening Letter Found in Hallway." *Telegram and Gazette*, April 24, 2007: B3.

Csikszentmihalyi, Mihaly. *Creativity: Flow and the Psychology of Discovery and Invention*. New York: Harper Collins, 1996.

Cullen-DuPont, Kathryn. "The Encyclopedia of Women's History in America." 332. New York: Facts on File, Incorporated, 2000.

Cummins, Jim. *Negotiating Identities: Education for Empowerment in a Diverse Society*. Ontario: California Association for Bilingual Education., 1996.

Daughters of the American Revolution. *The First School House in Worcester: Where John Adams Taught from 1755–1758.* Worcester: Commonwealth Press, 1903.

Dayal, Priyanka. "Barren Burncoat Landscape Toured." *Telegram and Gazette,* August 6, 2009: B3.

———. "Changing Faces." *Telegram and Gazette,* April 10, 2011: A1.

Del Prete, Thomas. *Improving the Odds: Developing Powerful Teaching Practice and a Culture of Learning in Urban High Schools.* New York: Teachers College Press, 2010.

Della Valle, Paul. "New GBV Foot Patrols Seeks a Toe Hold against Drugs." *Telegram and Gazette,* June 7, 1990: 1, 6.

———. "Valley Residents Recall the Riots and the 'reforms.'" *Telgeram and Gazette,* June 20, 1989: A4.

Dewey, John. *Democracy and Education.* New York: Macmillan, 1916.

DeWit, David J., Kim Karioja, and B. J. Rye. "Student Perceptions of Diminished Teacher and Classmate Support Following the Transition to High School: Are They Related to Declining Attendance?" *School Effectiveness and School Improvement: An International Journal of Research, Policy and Practice,* 2010: 451–72.

Doolan, Robert. "GBV Residents Air Grievances." *Telegram and Gazette,* July 20, 1990: A3.

Duckett, Richard. "GBV Health Center Takes Services to the People." *Telegram and Gazette,* June 25, 1995: B4.

Eames, Russel B. "GBV Panel Hears from Youth." *Worcester Telegram,* June 13, 1979: 3, 12.

——— "GBV Residents Look for Answers to Police Actions." *Telegram and Gazette,* July 20, 1990: A3.

———. "GBV Wants to Ease Tension; More Scuffles Spur Call for Meeting." *Telegram and Gazette,* July 20, 1990: A1.

———. "GBV Improving, Image Isen't Counselors Hear." *Worcester Telegram,* December 2, 1983.

Eberling, Eric R. "Massachusetts Education Laws of 1642, 1647, and 1648." In *Historical Dictionary of American Education,* by Richard J. Altenbaugh. Greenwood Press, 1999.

Echegaray, Chris. "Student Arrested After Firing Pellet Gun; Teachers, Administrators Cars Damaged." *Telegram and Gazette,* March 5, 2004: A1.

Editorial Staff. "Tensions at Great Brook." *Evening Gazette,* May 31, 1979.

Elkind, David. *Ties That Stress: The New Family Imbalance.* Cambridge, MA: Harvard University Press, 1994.

Evening Gazette. "Police Patrol Starts at Burncoat Schools." January 29, 1974: 21, 22.

———. "Policeman Committed to Hospital." June 23, 1979: 1.

———. "Survey Shows 643 Nonwhites in Schools." April 2, 1964: 1.

———. "Two Students Arrested in Burncoat St. Incident." January 29, 1974: 13, 14.

Fisher, Ericka. "Black Student Achievement and the Oppositional Culture Model." *Journal of Negro Education,* 2005: 201–9.

Fletcher, Edward. *City Document No. 57, 1902.* Worcester: Press of Charles Hamilton, 1903.

Fredricks, Jennifer A., Phyllis C. Blumenfeld, and Alison H. Paris. "School Engagement: Potential of the Concept, State of the Evidence." *Review of Educational Research*, 2004: 59–109.

Freid, Lawrence. "Worcester's First Junior-Senior High School." *Sunday Telegram*, July 27, 1952: 12–13.

Gaganakis, Margie. "Identity Construction in Adolescent Girls: The Context Dependency of Racial and Gendered Perceptions." *Gender and Education*, 2006: 361–79.

Gallagher, Ernest J. "Four Hurt in GBV Melee." *Worcester Telegram*, May 29, 1979: 1, 8.

Gandara, Patricia, and Frances Contreras. *The Latino Education Crisis: The Consequences of Failed Social Policies.* Cambridge, MA: Harvard University Press, 2009.

Griffin, George B. "Near-Riot at GBV Leads to 16 Arrests." *Telegram and Gazette*, July 18, 1990: A1.

———. "Storm Erupts at Police HQ; Fight Breaks Out After New Arrest." *Telegram and Gazette*, July 19, 1990: A1.

———. "WHA to Fund Police at GBV." *Telegram and Gazette*, February 8, 1992: 3.

Grogan-Taylor, Andrew, and Michael Woolley. "Protective Family Factors in the Context of Neighborhood: Promoting Positive Outcomes." *Family Relations*, 2006: 93–104.

Hammel, Lee. "Teen Shot in Chest; Victim Hit at GBV." *Telegram and Gazette*, August 2, 2004: B1.

———. "GBV Residents Meet; Disturbance Discussed; No-Shows Criticized." *Telegram and Gazette*, July 27, 1990: A3.

———. "Police Descend on GBV; Tactical Force Quiets Streets." *Telegram and Gazette*, August 19, 2002: A1.

———. "U.S. Official to Attend GBV Meeting." *Telegram and Gazette*, July 26, 1990: A3.

———. "Evaluation Irks Officials." *Worcester Telegram*, May 9, 1980: 3, 11.

———. "Sonia Ventura Slate Wins GBV Election." *Worcester Telegram*, April 8, 1981.

Harper, Charles A. *A Century of Public Teacher Education.* Westport, CT: Greenwood Press, 1970.

Hudley, Cynthia, Annette Daoud, Ted Polanco, and Rosi Wright-Castro. *Student Engagement, School Climate, and Future Expectations in High School.* Tampa, April 24, 2003.

Jefferson, Thomas. "A Bill for the More General Diffusion of Knowledge." In *Crusade Against Ignorance: Thomas Jefferson on Education*, by Gordon Lee, 83–92. New York: Teachers College Press, 1779.

Jencks, Christopher, and Susan Mayer. "The Social Consequences of Growing Up in a Poor Neighborhood." In *Inner-City Poverty in the United States*, edited by Laurence Lynn and Michael McGeary, 111–86. Washington, DC: National Academy Press, 1990.

Jennings, John., ed. *National Issues in Education; Elementary and Secondary Education Act.* Bloomington, IN: Phi Delta Kappa International, 1995.

Kendrick, Stephen, and Paul Kendrick. *Sarah's Long Walk: The Free Blacks of Boston and How Their Struggle For Equality Changed America.* Boston: Beacon Press, 2004.

Kotin, Lawrence, and William Aikman. *Legal Foundations of Compulsory Education.* New York: National University Publications, Kennikat Press, 1980.

Kotsopoulos, Nick. "Gardella Says Youth Curfew Isn't Justified." *Telegram and Gazette,* October 10, 1997: B1.

———. "GBV Health Center Plan Backed." *Telegram and Gazette,* June 3, 1996: 1.

———. "Council Oks Cutting GBV Security Force." *Worcester Telegram,* March 17, 1982: 1.

League of Women Voters. *Let's Look at Our Schools: A Survey of the Public Schools of Worcester Massachusetts.* Worcester, MA: Krizick & Corrigan, 1964.

Lewis, Diane. "Anger and Frustration Erupt at GBV." *Worcester Telegram,* June 22, 1979: 3, 11.

———. "Probers Hear Last Testimony." *Worcester Telegram,* June 21, 1979: 3, 13.

Lilyestrom, Betty. "6th Graders Study Spanish at Freeland St." *Worcester Telegram,* February 4, 1960: 21.

Limited English Proficiency. "Overview of Executive Order 13166." *Limited English Proficiency.* August 11, 2000. www.lep.gov/13166/eo13166.html (accessed November 8, 2011).

Lincoln, William. *History of Worcester, Massachusetts.* Worcester, MA: Charles Hersey, 1862.

Lopez, Marc Hugo. *Latinos and Education: Explaining the Attainment Gap.* Washington, DC: Pew Hispanic Center, 2009.

Lynch, David. "Burncoat High Gets Accreditation." *Evening Gazette,* November 10, 1969: 17.

Maguire, Karen, and Dave Mawson. "Burncoat Altercation is Probed." *Worcester Telegram,* October 7, 1983: 1, 4.

Mann, Horace. "On Education and National Welfare, 1848." In *History of the United States political system,* by Daniel J. Tichenor and Richard A. Harris, 416. Santa Brabara, CA: ABC CLIO, 2010.

Massachusetts Department of Elementary and Secondary Education. "2011 Mobility Rates." *Massachusetts Department of Elementay and Secondary Education.* 2011. profiles.doe.mass.edu/mobility/default.aspx?orgcode=03480503&fycode=2011&o rgtypecode=6& (accessed July 24, 2012).

———. "Burncoat Senior High—2011 Accountability Data." *Massachusetts Department of Elementary and Secondary Education.* 2011. profiles.doe.mass.edu /ayp/ayp_report/school.aspx?linkid=31&orgcode=03480503&orgtypecode=6& (accessed July 24, 2012).

———. "Cohort 2010 Graduation Rates." *Massachusetts Department of Elementary and Secondary Education.* 2010. profiles.doe.mass.edu/grad/grad_report.aspx?org code=03480503&orgtypecode=6&&fycode=2010 (accessed July 24, 2012).

———. "Education Reform Act of 1993." *Massachusetts Department of Elementary and Secondary Education.* June 6, 1993. archives.lib.state.ma.us /actsResolves/1993/1993acts0071.pdf (accessed January 5, 2012).

———. "Indicators (2010–2011)." *Massachusetts Department of Elementary and Secondary Education.* 2011. profiles.doe.mass.edu/profiles/student.aspx?orgcode=03480503&orgtypecode=6&leftNavId=303& (accessed July 24, 2012).

Mattingly, Paul. *The Classless Profession: American Schoolmen in the Nineteenth Century.* New York: New York University Press, 1975.

Mayberry, David T. "Home is What You Make It, So She Made It." *Evening Gazette,* August 17, 1986: 13.

———. "WHA 'Sells' Projects to Reluctant Public." *Evening Gazette,* August 17, 1986: 1, 2.

McDuffy v. Secretary of the Executive Office of Education. 415 Mass. 545 (Supreme Judicial Court for Suffolk County, June 1993).

McFarlane, Clive. "Small Schools Opposed at Burncoat; Faculty Says no to Plan Extension." *Telegram and Gazette,* April 19, 2005: B1.

———. "Talk of Repealing Desegregation Law // City School Officials Warn of Costs." *Telegram and Gazette,* April 18, 1996: A1.

———. "WHA Report Shocks Officials; Three Youth Gangs Reportedly Operate At Great Brook Valley." *Telegram and Gazette,* September 19, 1993: B3.

McHugh, Edward. "Projects Not Concentration Camps." *Worcester Telegram,* February 5, 1960: 19.

McLoyd, Vonnie C. "Socioeconomic Disadvantage and Child Development." *American Psychologist,* 1998: 185–204.

McNiff, Brian S. "Burncoat Mediation Program Scores $20k." *Telegram and Gazette,* October 5, 1999: B1.

———. "Students Give Legal Authorities a Piece of their Minds: Peer Mediation Credited with Helping Keep Peace at Burncoat." *Telegram and Gazette,* October 29, 1999: A2.

McQuillan, Patrick, and Yves Salomon-Fernandez. "The Impact of State Intervention on 'underperforming' Schools in Massachusetts: Implications for Policy and Practice." *Education Policy Analysis Archives,* 2008: 18.

Melady, Mark. "GBV Playground Plans Stir 'neglect' Charge." *Telegram and Gazette,* November 5, 1998: B1, B3.

———. "Man Shot at GBV; Officers Deployed." *Telegram and Gazette,* August 18, 2003: B1.

———. "New GBV Playground is Hailed." *Telegram and Gazette,* June 18, 1999: 1.

Milson, Andrew J. *Readings In American Educational Thought: From Puritanism to Progressivism.* Greenwich: Information Age Publishing, 2004.

Monahan, John J. "GBV Trash Bins are Off Limits to Firefighters." *Evening Gazette,* March 1, 1988: 11.

Mondale, Sarah, and Sarah Patton. *School: The Story of American Public Education.* Boston, MA: Beacon, 2001.

Nangle, Richard. "Police to Escort Buses at GBV // Shooting Probed." *Telegram and Gazette,* April 18, 1996: B1.

Nason, Rev. Elias. "An Excerpt from Gazetteer of Massachusetts." *City of Worcester.* 1873. www.worcesterma.gov/city-clerk/history/general/excerpt-from-gazetteer-of-massachusetts (accessed December 1, 2011).

National Center for Education Statistics. "Projections of Education Statistics to 2017." *U.S. Department of Education, Insitute of Education Sciences.* 2008. nces.ed.gov /programs/projections2017/tables/table_32.asp.

———. "The Condition of Education 2010." *U.S. Department of Education, Institute of Education Sciences.* 2010. nces.ed.gov/pubs2010/2010028.pdf.

Neild, Ruth Curran, and Robert Balfanz. "An Extreme Degree of Difficulty: The Educational Demographics of Urban Neighborhood High Schools." *Journal of Education for Students Placed at Risk,* 2006: 123–41.

Newmann, Fred. *Student Engagement and Achievement in American Secondary Schools.* New York: Teachers College Press, 1992.

Newton, Kimberly. "Report is against Forced Desegregation." *Telegram and Gazette,* November 19, 1989: B1.

Noguera, Pedro A. *City Schools and the American Dream: Reclaiming the Promise of Public Education.* New York: Teacher's College Press, 2003.

Nutt, Charles. *History of Worcester and its People.* New York: Lewis Historical Publishing Company, 1919.

Oakes, Jeannie. *Keeping Track: How Schools Structure Inequality.* New Haven: Yale University Press, 2005.

Oakes, Jeannie, and Martin Lipton. *Teaching to Change the World.* New York: Mcgraw-Hill, 2007.

Ogbu, John. "Minority Coping Responses and School Experience." *The Journal of Psychohistory,* 1991: 433–56.

Ogbu, John U., and Signithia Fordham. "Black students' School Success: Coping with the 'Burden' of 'Acting White.'" *Urban Review,* 1986: 176–206.

Orfield, Gary, Erica Frakenberg, and Liliana M Garces. "Statement of American Social Scientists of Research on School Desegregation to the U.S. Supreme Court in *Parents v. Seattle School District and Meredithv.* Jefferson County." *Urban Review,* 2008: 96–136.

Ornstein, Allan. *Teaching and Schooling in America.* New York: Allyn and Bacon, 2003.

Ornstein, Allan, Daniel Levine, and Gerald Gutek. *Foundations of Education, 11th Edition.* Belmont, CA: Wadsworth Publishing, 2010.

Orr, Amy. "Black-White Differences in Achievement: The Importance of Wealth." *Sociology of Education,* 2003: 281–304.

Palardy, J Michael. "The Effects of Teacher Expectations on Children's Literacy Development." *Reading Improvement,* 1998: 184–86.

Peterson, Merrill D., ed. *Thomas Jefferson: Writings.* New York: Library of America, 1984.

Popkin, Susan J., Gregory Acs, and Robin E. Smith. *The Urban Institute's Program on Neighborhoods and Youth Development: Understanding How Place Matters for Kids.* Washington, DC: The Urban Institute, 2009.

Ream, Robert. "Toward Understanding How Social Capital Mediates the Impact of Student Mobility on Mexican American Achievement." *Social Forces,* 2005: 201–24.

Reis, Jacqueline. "12 Not Returning to Burncoat After Brawl; 3 Others of 15 Charged are Back at School; Everythings been Calm, Student Says." *Telegram and Gazette,* Novemeber 19, 2005: A3.

———. "Burncoat Principal, Parents Speak Out on Fight, Safety." *Telegram and Gazette*, November 2, 2005: A1.

———. "Fight among Burncoat Students Leads to Injuries and 11 Arrests; Dispute Grows into Melee Involving 60." *Telegram and Gazette*, October 20, 2005: A1.

———. "On with the Show." *Telegram and Gazette*, November 15, 2008: A3.

———. "Police to Continue Patrols at Burncoat." *Telegram & Gazette*, October 22, 2005: A2.

Roderick, Melissa. "What's Happening to the Boys? Early High School Experiences and School Outcomes Among African American Male Adolescents in Chicago." *Urban Education*, 2003: 538–607.

Rollock, Nicola. "Why Black Girls Don't Matter: Exploring How Race and Gender Shape Academic Success in an Inner City School." *Support for Learning*, 2007: 197–202.

Roscigno, Vincent. "Race and the Reproduction of Educational Disadvantage." *Social Forces*, 1998: 1033–61.

Rushford, David J. "Historical Highlights of Worcester." *City of Worcester.* www.worcesterma.gov/uploads/2e/a9/2ea982935ba5e18ead6b31f4aa9cf94d /historical-highlights.pdf (accessed January 4, 2012).

Sampson, Robert J, Jeffrey D. Morenoff, and Stephen Raudenbush. "Social Anatomy of Racial and Ethnic Disparities in Violence." *American Journal of Public Health*, 2005: 224–32.

Sandrof, Ivan. "What It's Like Living in Great Brook Valley Gardens." *Worceter Telegram*, May 1, 1955: 17–18.

Schultz, Stanley K. *The Culture Factory: Boston Public Schools, 1789–1860.* New York: Oxford University Press, 1973.

Sehgal, Neetu. "New Center Reaches Out to Youngsters." *Telegram and Gazette*, July 14, 2000: B1.

Shaunessy, Elizabeth, and Patricia Alzarez McHatton. "Urban Students' Perceptions of Teachers: Views of Students in General, Special, and Honors Education." *Urban Review*, 2009: 486–503.

Shaw, Kathleen A. "GBV Vents Complaints: Residents Seek Official Help to Fight Crime." *Telegram and Gazette*, November 3, 2000: B1.

———. "Worcester Police Arrest 11 Participants in 3 Melees." *Telegram and Gazette*, May 16, 2000: B3.

———. "Youths Pelt Vehicles in GBV." *Telegram and Gazette*, August 25, 1993: A1.

Sheehan, Nancy. "Closed GBV Meeting is Called Productive." *Telegram and Gazette*, August 3, 1990: A3.

Shernoff, David J., and Jennifer A. Schmidt. "Further Evidence of an Engagement-Achievement Paradox Among U.S. High School Students." *J Youth Adolescence*, 2008: 564–80.

Shipton, Clifford K. "Harvard, Yale, and the Educated Colonial." *Michigan Quarterly Review*, 1968: 177–82.

Shulkin, Jeremy. "Person of the Year." *Worcester Magazine*, December 28, 2012: 8–14.

Siann, Gerda, Pauline Lightbody, Ruth Stocks, and David Walsh. "Motivation and Attribution at Secondary School: The Role of Ethnic Group and Gender." *Gender and Education*, 1996: 261–74.

Simmons, Richard C. "Early Massachusetts: A Puritan Commonwealth." *History Today*, 1968: 259–67.

Sizer, Theodore. *Horace's compromise*. Boston: Houghton Mifflin, 1985.

Smith, Jacquelyn. *Forbes*. January 17, 2012. www.forbes.com/sites/jacquelynsmith /2012/01/17/the-happiest-and-unhappiest-cities-to-work-in/ (accessed February 1, 2012).

Southwick, Albert B. "The Lessons of history." *Inside Worcester*, August 1990: 20–26.

Spring, Joel. *The American School 1642–2004*. New York: McGraw Hill, 2005.

Sullivan, Peter. *City Document No. 74, 1919*. Worcester: Commonwealth Press, 1920.

Sumner, Charles, and Massachusetts. Supreme Judicial Court. *Argument of Charles Sumner, Esq., against the Constitutionality of Separate Colored Schools: In the Case of Sarah C. Roberts vs. The City of Boston*. Boston: B.F. Roberts, 1849.

Sunday Telegram. "Evaluation Gives High Rating to Burncoat Magnet Program." August 17, 1986: 33A.

———. "Good Times at GBV." August 20, 1998: B1.

———. "McGrath Seeks Funds to Police Housing Projects." June 15, 1975: 4.

———. "Tension Reported High 'Incident Feared' at GBV." February 11, 1979: 23A.

Swail, Watson Scott, Alberto Cabrera, and Chul Lee. *Laitna/o youth and the pathway to college*. Washington, DC: Education Policy Institute, 2004.

Taylor, April Z., and Sandra Graham. "An Examination of the Relationship Between Achievement Values and Perceptions of Barriers Among Low-SES African American and Latino Students." *Journal of Educational Psychology*, 2007: 52–64.

The Commission for Latino Educational Excellence. *Creating the Will: A Community Roadmap to Achieving Excellence for Latino Students in Worcester*. Worcester: Worcester State University, Latino Education Institute, 2011.

The Evening Gazette. "Burncoat High Opens with 775 Attending." December 7, 1964: 18.

Tolman, Lynne. "GBV Residents Rap Police Overreaction." *Telegram and Gazette*, July 18, 1990: A1.

US Census Bureau. *United States Census 2010*, 2010. census.gov/2010census/ (accessed January 2, 2012).

US Department of Education. *No Child Left Behind*. 2001. www2.ed.gov/policy /elsec/leg/esea02/index.html (accessed January 5, 2012).

———. *Strengthening No Child Left Behind*. www2.ed.gov/nclb/overview/intro /reauth/index.html (accessed January 5, 2012).

Valencia, Milton J. "Crime Declines at GBV, Curtis; WHA Director Cites New Housing Policy." *Telegram and Gazette*, February 9, 2005: B1.

———. "Curtis Apts. Getting Face-Lift ; $20M Targets Quality of Life." *Telegram and Gazette*, May 5, 2006: B1.

Ward, Janie Victoria. *The Skin We're In: Teaching our Children to be Emotionally Strong*. New York: Free Press, 2000.

Watras, Joseph. "Education and Evangelism in the English Colonies." *American Educational History Journal*, 2008: 205–19.

Waxman, Hersh C., Yolanda N. Padron, and Jon P. Gray. *Educational Resiliency: Student, Teacher, and School Perspectives*. Greenwich: Information Age Publishing, 2004.

Weiner, Bernard. "History of Motivational Research in Education." *Journal of Educational Psychology*, 1990: 616–22.

Williamson, Dianne. "GBV Cleans House of Drug Dealers." *Telegram and Gazette*, March 18, 1990: B1.

———. "Near-Riot Dispersed at GBV." *Telegram and Gazette*, July 18, 1990: A1.

Wolfe, Kevin. "Police Brutality Called Root of Problems at GBV." *Worcester Telegram*, July 12, 1979: 1, 13.

Worcester Evening Post. "Schools of Yesterday and Today." July 1, 1922: 6, 8.

Worcester Historical Society. "Internet Archive." *Collections, Book 1.* 1722–39. www.archive.org/stream/worcecollections02worcuoft/worcecollections02 worcuoft_djvu.txt (accessed August 10, 2011).

Worcester Public Schools. *Burncoat High School-Instructional Focus.* Worcester, 2011.

Worcester Regional Chamber of Commerce. 2012. www.worcesterchamber.org /worcester-named-one-of-five-best-housing-markets-in-country (accessed February 5, 2012).

Worcester Telegram. "Burncoat High Adds Grade." February 11, 1983: 3A.

———. "Burncoat to Get a $20,000 Foundation Grant." Ocotber 5, 1982: 3A.

———. "GBV Violence Follows Slaying." June 22, 1979: 3.

———. "Rent-Subsidy Program is Favored." September 23, 1967: 23.

Wright, George. *City Document No. 67, 1912.* Worcester: Belisle Printing and Publishing, 1913.

Index

ability tracking, 14, 39–43, *41*, 54–55
Adams, John, 5–6
adequate yearly progress (AYP), 51
adolescence, 75–77
advanced placement (AP), 39, 41, 88
African American students:
    achievement and, 65–68; at
    Burncoat Senior High School,
    40, 60–61, 67–68, 78–79, 80–86;
    segregation and, 8–9, 14–15, 17–18,
    39–40
Allende, Angel Luis, 29
Ansalone, George, 40
Asian Longhorn Beetle, 24
athletic teams, 39
attribution theory, 79–80
Ayers, William, xvii

Balfanz, Robert, 21
Banks, James, 105
Bedford Heights (Worcester), 23–24
believing, 100–102
Bell, Bethany A., xv
Benard, Bonnie, 99
bilingual and English language
    learners, 16, 39, 59
Bilingual Education Act (1968), 16
bilingual teachers, 59
Board of Education (Massachusetts),
    7–8

Boone, Melinda: on equality, 54–55;
    on faith, 94; on future of public
    schools, 98, 99; on MERA, 44–45;
    on NCLB, 51; power relations and,
    47; on socioeconomic status, 71–74;
    on tracking, 42–43
Bourdieu, Pierre, xv, 21
Brofenbrenner, Urie, 33
Brown v. Board of Education, 9,
    14–15
Burncoat Senior High School
    (Worcester): academic engagement
    at, 78; deviant behaviors and
    punishments at, 37–38; drop-out
    rate at, 37; educational policies at,
    43–45; extracurricular activities
    at, 39; funding for, 39; graduation
    rate at, 38; guidance counselors
    at, 89–90; High School Survey
    of Student Engagement and, 35;
    history of, 16–17; mobility rate at,
    36–37; neighborhood and, 23–33;
    No Child Left Behind and, 48–53,
    74, 93; population of, 35–36,
    36; racial unrest and tensions at,
    60–61; relationships with teachers
    at, 76–77, 80–89, 91–93; safety
    and, 38; socioeconomic status and,
    69–73; student teacher ratio at,
    38–39; suspension rates at, 37–38;

About the Author

Ericka J. Fisher is associate professor of education and chair at the College of the Holy Cross. Primarily focusing on multicultural education, educational psychology, and academic achievement, her published works examine the experiences of vulnerable populations in American secondary schools.